Concord Cunningham
Coast to Coast

THE

Scripture
Sleuth 4

By
Mathew Halverson

Concord Cunningham Coast To Coast:
The Scripture Sleuth 4
Mathew Halverson

Cover Design by Melanie Schmidt
Cover Illustration by Don Stewart

Truck shown on the cover is actual vehicle used to deliver the 2003 Capitol Christmas tree from Idaho to Washington, D.C. For more information visit www.capitolholidaytree2003.org. Photo courtesy USDA Forest Service. No copyright.

ISBN 1-885904-53-3

PRINTED IN THE UNITED STATES OF AMERICA
by
FOCUS PUBLISHING
Bemidji, Minnesota 56601

CONCORD CUNNINGHAM
COAST TO COAST

THE

Scripture
Sleuth 4

For my sister, Holly,
who travels near and far for God's work.

Contents

Locations of Chapter Mysteries in
Concord Cunningham Coast To Coast:
The Scripture Sleuth 4

Chapter	Location
1. The Painted Pine	Pine Tops area (NW Washington)
2. The City Sign Bandit	Pine Tops area (NW Washington)
3. The Disappearing Dog Walker	Idaho side of Idaho/Montana border
4. The Ice Fish Shack	In Montana, between Bozeman and Billings
5. The Super Spill	In South Dakota, just past the Missouri River on I-90
6. Taste Test Troubles	In Iowa, near Des Moines on I-80
7. Lamp Love	Eastern Illinois
8. The Great Turtle Race	Eastern Indiana, along I-70
9. Breakdown Blues	Eastern Ohio, along I-70
10. The Jumbo Jugglers	Western Maryland, along I-68
11. Welcome to Washington, D.C.	Washington, D.C.
12. Big Bounce Shoes	Pine Tops Airport

1
THE
PAINTED PINE

Pine Tops was a long way from Washington, D.C. And Pine Tops was so small that most people in the nation's capital and everywhere else had never even heard it. But that was about to change.

Each year, one tree in America was chosen to be the Capitol Christmas Tree. The chosen tree would be cut down and taken to Washington, D.C. There it would be decorated and displayed on the lawn of the United States Capitol building. And out of the millions of pine trees in the United States, the tree chosen to be this year's Capitol Christmas Tree was in the forest next to Pine Tops!

The big news had been announced only a few days ago. Already, reporters from national television networks were arriving in Pine Tops. They wanted to be sure they had their cameras rolling when the Capitol Christmas Tree was cut down and loaded onto a semi-truck

In just a short time, the small Pacific Northwest town had become famous. But Pine Tops had one other claim to fame that not too many outsiders knew about. It was the home of the world's best Scripture Sleuth. His name was Concord Cunningham.

Concord could solve mysteries that no one else could. And, as most people in Pine Tops knew, Concord didn't use fancy computer programs or secret spy gear. He used his Bible and his brain. No matter what the mystery was,

Concord could find a clue in the Bible that would help him crack the case.

Concord also knew how to find his way into the middle of the most exciting events in Pine Tops. He stuck by his father's side. Mr. Cunningham worked for the local newspaper, the *Ponderosa Press*. As the newspaper's top reporter, Mr. Cunningham was always asked to cover the biggest stories in Pine Tops. And there had never been a bigger story than the Capitol Christmas Tree.

"Is it true that the forest service has kept the location of the tree a secret?" Concord asked his dad. They were driving through town.

"Yep," his dad said with a nod. "They didn't want anyone to bother the tree before it gets cut down later today." Mr. Cunningham's cell phone rang as he turned a corner. He pulled the car over to the side of the road and reached for his phone. Then he opened his reporter's notepad as he answered.

"Hello," the tall reporter answered. "Really? Fantastic!" He pulled out his pen and took a few notes. "Okay, we're on our way." He pushed a button to end the call and turned to his slim, sandy-haired son. "Concord, how would you like to be one of the first people to see the Capitol Christmas Tree?" Mr. Cunningham asked with a smile.

"I'd love it!" Concord answered excitedly.

"That was my editor," Mr. Cunningham explained. "The forest service just told the media the location of the tree. They gave us a one hour head start."

"What do you mean?" Concord asked.

Mr. Cunningham pulled back into traffic. "In one hour, the forest service will tell the public the location of the tree. Then everyone will be able to come to the ceremony later today when the tree is cut down."

"Why do the reporters get to go first?" Concord asked.

"It's just like football or basketball games," his dad answered. "The reporters get to go early to set up cameras and that sort of thing."

"Is Uncle Joe going to be there, too?" Concord asked. Mr. Cunningham's brother, Joe, and his family had moved to Pine Tops two months ago. Uncle Joe was the new photographer at the *Ponderosa Press*.

"I'm sure he'll be there," Mr. Cunningham said with a grin. "You know your uncle. He'd never miss a chance for a great picture. The only question is what crazy place he'll take his pictures from this time. I think he's still recovering from the cow milking picture."

Uncle Joe always tried to find the best possible angle for a picture. No matter what. Just a few days ago he was taking a picture of a farmer milking a cow. The best angle was from above, so Uncle Joe climbed onto the shoulders of a nearby bull. Unfortunately, Uncle Joe dropped his film bag on the bull's back, and then he got bucked seven feet into the air. But he got the picture.

Mr. Cunningham and Concord finished driving across town and turned onto the main highway going north. After passing the northern edge of town, it only took a few minutes to reach the snow line. As usual, the beginning of winter had brought some large snow storms to the Pine Tops area. Though the snow hadn't yet stuck in town, the surrounding mountains had plenty.

After about ten minutes on the highway, they turned east onto a plowed forest service road. They slowly drove through a narrow canyon with walls of plowed snow on both sides of the car. After another twenty minutes, they came into a white meadow. In the middle of the meadow was a big, beautiful pine tree. The tree was surrounded by a rope and orange construction cones resting on the snow.

"That must be the tree," Mr. Cunningham said as he parked the car.

"It's perfect," Concord said as he studied the tree's shape. The soaring pine was deep green and seemed to be flawless. Then Concord scanned the meadow. On the left side of the tree, a forest ranger was talking to a man who had been walking with show shoes. On the other side of the tree there was a stream. The stream was about twenty feet away from the tree, and it had not yet frozen for the winter.

The meadow was surrounded by thick forest. There were no buildings, fences, or signs of civilization in sight. But there were a couple of parked cars. One was a forest service truck, and the other was a car that Concord recognized. Next to the car was a girl. "There's Faith!" Concord said as he waved at her. She saw Concord and waved back.

Faith was Uncle's Joe's daughter, which made her Concord's cousin. She was one year older than Concord, one inch taller, and she had shoulder-length brown hair. She also paid more attention to details than anyone Concord had ever met.

"Hi Concord. Hi Uncle Bill," Faith said as she walked over to the Cunninghams' car. Concord and his dad both smiled and greeted her. As they got out of the car, Concord grabbed his backpack and Mr. Cunningham grabbed his reporter's notepad.

"I see you switched from a brown to a black notepad, Uncle Bill," Faith observed.

"Right you are," Mr. Cunningham said with a chuckle. As a reporter, he appreciated her keen eye for detail. "Is your dad already setting up for pictures, Faith?" Mr. Cunningham asked.

"He sure is," Faith said. She pointed toward the trees across the meadow.

Mr. Cunningham scanned the white forest floor. "All I see is snow," he mumbled.

"Look higher," Faith said.

Mr. Cunningham looked up into the trees and saw Uncle Joe waving. He had climbed about thirty feet up into a pine tree. As usual, Uncle Joe was wearing his favorite tan vest, which was loaded with pockets for all of his camera gear. He also wore a red stocking cap, which wasn't too surprising. His balding head got cold in the winter.

Concord noticed a slight wind, which had been causing the snow in the area to blow. It also caused Uncle Joe's tree to gently sway. "Wow! I hope he's hanging on tight," Concord said.

Faith nodded. "He's got a safety rope," she said.

Once Mr. Cunningham knew his brother was safe, he decided to get down to business. "It looks like we beat the rest of the reporters up here," he said. "Let's see if we can get the first interview with the forest ranger."

They all trudged through the deep snow to the ranger, who was still talking to the man with snowshoes. The ranger wore a green uniform and a matching green coat. The snowshoe man wore a yellow coat and pants and had brown tennis shoes strapped onto his snowshoes. Concord had never seen snowshoes this close. They reminded him of tennis rackets.

"Hello, gentlemen," Mr. Cunningham said. "I'm Bill Cunningham with the *Ponderosa Press*."

"Hello, Mr. Cunningham," the ranger said. "I'm Ed Green, and this is Rick Dudley." They all shook hands. "And these must be your kids," Ranger Green said as he nodded at Concord and Faith.

"Concord is my son," Mr. Cunningham said as he put his hand on Concord's shoulder. "And Faith is my niece. Her dad is a photographer for our paper, and he's right up there." Mr. Cunningham pointed across the meadow and up into the trees. Uncle Joe noticed everyone looking at him and waved. The group waved back.

"I hope he's not afraid of heights," the ranger joked.

"I don't think he's afraid of anything when it comes to taking pictures," Mr. Cunningham answered. Then he flipped open his notepad and decided to ask the first question. "Ranger Green, I understood that the location of the tree was a secret. How did Mr. Dudley know where it was?"

"Mr. Dudley was taking a snowshoe walk through this area at dawn," the ranger replied.

"You've been out here since dawn?" Mr. Cunningham asked.

Mr. Dudley nodded. "It's been a long morning," he said.

Faith observed that he had no backpack or supplies. He had only his clothes and snowshoes. "You must be hungry," she said.

"I am," Mr. Dudley answered. "All of my things are at my car, which is parked a couple miles from here. But I knew I couldn't leave until other people got here. The tree had to be kept safe."

"What do you mean?" Mr. Cunningham asked.

"I was walking along the edge of this meadow at sunrise," Mr. Dudley began. "I saw the big tree with ropes around it in the middle of the meadow, and I knew it had to be the Capitol Christmas Tree."

"So the ropes were already up at dawn?" Mr. Cunningham asked Ranger Green.

The ranger nodded. "We put them up yesterday," he answered.

Mr. Dudley continued his story. "As I got closer to the tree, I noticed a man next to it. He had a big bucket of white paint, and he was throwing the paint on the tree. He was trying to ruin it!"

Concord's jaw dropped. "Why would anyone do that?" he asked.

"I don't know," Mr. Dudley replied. "But I knew I had to stop him. So I started yelling at him from across the meadow. He saw me, and I think he got scared. He grabbed his bucket of paint, jumped into his truck, and drove off."

Concord and Faith walked up to the rope that guarded the tree. They studied the tree's branches. "I don't see any white paint on the tree," Faith said.

"That's because our friend Mr. Dudley is a national hero," Ranger Green said with a smile. "He saved the tree!"

"What did you do?" Mr. Cunningham asked.

"I realized that if the paint dried on the tree it would be impossible to get off," Mr. Dudley said. "All the painted branches would need to be cut off, and then the tree would look awful. So I knew I didn't have much time. I tried wiping the paint off with snow, but that didn't work. Then I saw the stream." Mr. Dudley pointed beyond the other side of the tree.

"So," Mr. Dudley continued, "I went over there for some water to wash the paint off the tree. It took quite a few trips because there was so much paint on the tree, but it worked!"

Concord looked at the base of the tree, expecting to see wet snow and snowshoe prints from all of Mr. Dudley's work. However, the wind had been causing a snow drift to accumulate there all morning. It covered up everything underneath. The drifting snow had also covered most of the meadow, so no one could check the foot tracks or tire tracks in the snow to see if Mr. Dudley's story was true.

"It sounds as if you are a hero, Mr. Dudley," Mr. Cunningham said as he scribbled a few notes. "I'm sure you realize that all the reporters coming this way are going to want to interview you. You might become famous for a while."

"I know," Mr. Dudley said with a big smile. "I'm happy I was able to save the day."

Mr. Cunningham and the two men began walking toward Uncle Joe. Mr. Cunningham knew that his editor would want Mr. Dudley's picture for the newspaper. Meanwhile, Concord dropped his backpack to the snow and pulled out his Bible. Something about Mr. Dudley's story was bothering him. He flipped to the concordance section of his Bible and started looking up verses.

"What are you doing, Concord?" Faith asked.

"I'm not sure that Mr. Dudley's story is true," Concord replied.

"Do you think he made up the story so everyone would think he's a hero?" Faith asked.

Concord tapped on a verse and looked up with a grin. "I'm almost positive," he said as he scratched his chin. "But I have a question for you. Were Mr. Dudley's shoes dry or wet?"

Faith looked at Mr. Dudley in the distance. Then she closed her eyes to remember all the details about him that she had observed. "Dry," she answered. "I remember thinking that his snowshoes really did keep his feet out of the snow because his tennis shoes were dry." She opened her eyes and looked curiously at Concord. "Do you think his shoes should have been wet from walking over to the stream so much?"

"Not exactly," Concord answered. "Here," he said as he handed Faith his Bible. "Read John 4:11. I need to go tell my dad that Mr. Dudley isn't a hero at all."

How did Concord know that Mr. Dudley's story wasn't true?

Read John 4:11 for the clue that Concord gave Faith.

The solution to "The Painted Pine" is on page 98.

2
THE CITY SIGN BANDIT

The *Ponderosa Press* had never been busier. Newspaper sales doubled when Mr. Cunningham's stories about the Capitol Christmas Tree began appearing. As more newspapers sold, more Pine Tops businesses wanted to advertise in the paper. So the *Ponderosa Press* decided to continue printing stories about the tree for as long as possible.

After a big meeting with all the editors, the newspaper staff decided to ask Mr. Cunningham to follow the tree all the way to Washington, D.C. His assignment would be to send back stories each day as the tree made its way east. Uncle Joe was asked to go, too, so he could take pictures of the tree in different places across the country.

Mr. Cunningham was surprised. He had never been sent such a great distance on a story for the *Ponderosa Press*. But that wasn't the biggest surprise of the day in the Cunningham house. The biggest shock was that Mr. Cunningham and Uncle Joe had invited Concord and Faith to come, too! The two Cunningham dads were proud of their kids for exposing Mr. Dudley's lie about the painted tree, and they thought the trip would be a nice reward.

Normally the dads would have considered inviting other family members, too. However, no one else was able to come. Concord's brother was going to be busy with sports practices, and his sister was sick with the chicken

CONCORD CUNNINGHAM COAST TO COAST: THE *Scripture Sleuth 4*

pox. So, Mrs. Cunningham would stay home with them. Faith's mom would be staying home, too, to take care of Faith's new baby brother.

The trip came at a perfect time. School had just been released for Thanksgiving break. The trip to Washington, D.C. would take about a week, which was the length of the break.

The trip also started at a strange time of day. Actually, it wasn't even day. It was eight o'clock at night!

"So why are we leaving tonight instead of tomorrow?" Concord asked as he brought his suitcase down the stairs.

"The tree is leaving tonight, and we're supposed to be with it every step of the way," Mr. Cunningham explained. "The tree is scheduled to stop in certain towns along its route east. It's kind of like a tour. Some towns are even planning to put the tree in special events like parades. I guess it needs to leave tonight to be on schedule."

Concord nodded and carried his suitcase across the living room. He and his dad said their goodbyes to the family, and they were out the door. Concord hurried over to the car in the driveway, but his dad was walking toward the dark street.

"Hey, Dad, we're not walking to Washington, D.C., are we?" Concord joked. As his eyes adjusted to the dark, Concord realized that his father was walking toward a van parked along the curb.

"This way, Concord," Mr. Cunningham called as he got to the van. He opened the van's door. "We've got new wheels for the week. The newspaper is renting this van for us. We'll drive it out east, and then we'll fly home."

"Cool!" Concord cried out as he hurried over to the van. The trip seemed to get more exciting by the minute.

A short while later they picked up Uncle Joe and Faith.

With Mr. Cunningham and Uncle Joe in the front, and Concord and Faith in the back, the group was ready to begin the big adventure.

However, as they were about to leave the city limits of Pine Tops, Mr. Cunningham slowed the van. Concord looked down the road and saw the red and white lights of Chief Riggins' patrol car flashing through the darkness. The patrol car was parked on the side of the road behind a pickup truck.

"It looks like the chief caught somebody speeding," Concord said.

Mr. Cunningham's brow tightened as they got closer to the patrol car. The van's headlights lit up the area, and Mr. Cunningham observed the scene. He saw that Chief Riggins wasn't standing by the truck or sitting in his patrol car. The chief was standing way off the road in the dirt. Mr. Cunningham knew this was unusual, and it certainly was not where the chief would be standing to issue a speeding ticket.

So Mr. Cunningham parked the van behind the chief's patrol car and whipped out his reporter's notepad.

"Do you think there's a story here?" Uncle Joe asked, quickly reaching for his camera.

"Could be," Mr. Cunningham answered. "Do you remember the report about the City Sign Bandit that we saw on the news wire a few days ago?"

"Oh yeah," said Uncle Joe. "He's the guy who's been stealing signs all across the Northwest. He always steals those signs that say 'Welcome to Pine Tops' or whatever the town is."

"Right," said Mr. Cunningham. Then he pointed at Chief Riggins. "Take a look at where the chief is standing."

Uncle Joe looked at the chief. "He's right by the Pine

13

Tops sign!" Uncle Joe gasped. "Do you think the chief just caught the City Sign Bandit?"

"I think we'd better find out," Mr. Cunningham answered. He reached for the van door, but then he paused. He flipped back seven or eight pages in his notepad. "I'm trying to remember why that report came across the news wire."

"What do you mean, Dad?" Concord asked from the back seat.

"The City Sign Bandit has been stealing signs for years," Mr. Cunningham explained. "There must have been a reason why the news wire mentioned him this week."

"Maybe he stole another sign," Faith said.

Mr. Cunningham nodded. Then he tapped his notepad. "You're right, Faith, but there's more," he said. "The police finally got a tip about the bandit's truck. An eye witness said the bandit's truck has a hood ornament that looks like a stop sign."

They all had a quick chuckle.

Concord had an idea. "Do you think this truck that Chief Riggins pulled over has the stop sign hood ornament?" he asked.

Mr. Cunningham thought for a moment. "If the bandit heard a news report about the tip, I'm sure he would have taken the hood ornament off his truck," he said. "But if he didn't hear about the report, the hood ornament might still be there. Let's go check it out!"

They jumped out of the van and hurried up the road to the front of the truck. They quickly discovered that the truck had no hood ornament. Mr. Cunningham tapped his notepad as he thought. A moment later, he said, "Let's go talk to the chief."

They all hurried across the shoulder of the road and

stepped across about twenty feet of dirt, rocks, and fallen pine needles to get to the chief. Chief Riggins looked the same as always. He was a plump man with a perfectly trimmed moustache and a freshly pressed uniform.

It was Chief Riggins who had given Concord the nickname "The Concordance" when the Scripture Sleuth had solved his first mystery. The nickname was quite fitting. Concord was an ace with the concordance at the back of his Bible. He used it to look up verses about ideas, words, and people in the Bible. The verses he found helped him answer questions and solve mysteries.

The group approached Chief Riggins, who was talking to a large man. The man wore a heavy red flannel shirt, blue jeans, and work boots. The chief and the man were standing next to the sign that welcomed drivers to Pine Tops.

Though the sign marked the official city limits of Pine Tops, it was at least a quarter of a mile from the first city street. The area was dark and mostly quiet, except for the noise of a passing car every now and then.

"Hello, Chief," Mr. Cunningham said as he raised his pen to his notepad. "Is there trouble with the Pine Tops sign?"

"I thought there was," Chief Riggins said. "This is Mr. Cain, and I almost arrested him for trying to steal it!"

"What happened?" Mr. Cunningham asked.

"I was driving down the highway on patrol," the chief replied. "When I drove by the sign, I noticed a truck parked next to it. So I stopped to check things out. I didn't see anyone around, but I noticed that two of the bolts holding the sign to its posts were taken out and lying on the ground. I started to wonder if the City Sign Bandit was trying to take our sign."

"Where was Mr. Cain?" Mr. Cunningham asked.

"I was hiding," Mr. Cain said. "I knew that Chief Riggins would probably think I was trying to steal the sign if he saw me."

"And were you trying to steal the sign?" Mr. Cunningham asked.

"Of course not!" Mr. Cain answered quickly. "I was trying to put it back."

Mr. Cunningham scratched his head in confusion. "Where was it?" he asked.

"The City Sign Bandit stole it!" Mr. Cain answered.

There was a moment of silence as the group let his words sink in. Then Mr. Cunningham continued his questions. "How did you get the sign back?" he asked.

Mr. Cain shook his head. "It was mostly luck," he began. "I was driving down the highway just up the road from here."

"And when was this?" Mr. Cunningham interrupted.

"About fifteen minutes ago," Mr. Cain replied. "A pick-up truck was coming down the highway from the opposite direction. As it drove by me, I noticed it had a funny hood ornament shaped like a stop sign. I remembered from a news report I had heard a while back that the City Sign Bandit had one of those. So I turned around and started to follow him. I honked my horn until he finally pulled over. Then he quickly jumped out and pulled something out of the back of his truck. He put it on the edge of the highway, and he sped away. I looked down and saw that he had left the Pine Tops sign!"

"Did you chase him?" Mr. Cunningham asked.

"I thought about it," Mr. Cain said. "But I didn't want to just leave the Pine Tops sign there on the side of the road. I loaded it into my truck. By the time I finished, I knew the bandit was long gone and I would never catch him. Instead, I brought the sign back here. The bandit had left the screws on the ground by the posts, so I got a wrench out of my truck and started putting the sign back on its posts. When I saw a car coming, I hid behind a tree. I didn't want the person to think I was the bandit. It turned out to be Chief Riggins. He got out of his car to check things out. It didn't take him long to find me."

"For a minute I thought I had found the City Sign Bandit," the chief said with a laugh. "Then Mr. Cain explained what happened."

Faith pulled Concord back from the group. "What if Mr. Cain was actually unscrewing the sign when the chief found him, and he just made up that whole story?" she whispered.

"It's possible," Concord whispered back, "but I don't know how we could prove which way he was turning his wrench." Concord rubbed his chin as he thought. "Maybe there's something else that we could prove." Concord ran back to the van and grabbed his backpack.

He pulled out his Bible and a flashlight and started flipping pages. A minute later he ran back to the group. "Chief, I think you did catch the City Sign Bandit," Concord announced. "Or at least somebody who was trying to steal the Pine Tops sign."

"What?" Mr. Cain exclaimed. "Didn't you listen to what happened?"

"I did," Concord said. "It was a good story, but it wasn't true." Concord turned to Chief Riggins. "Here, Chief," The Concordance said as he handed his Bible to the chief. "Read Acts 22:11. And then you'd better pull out your hand-cuffs."

How did Concord know that Mr. Cain's story wasn't true?

Read Acts 22:11 for the clue that Concord gave Chief Riggins.

The solution to "The City Sign Bandit" is on page 99.

3
THE
DISAPPEARING
DOG WALKER

"Is everybody buckled up?" Mr. Cunningham asked as he started the van's engine.

"Yep," said Uncle Joe in the passenger seat.

"I'm buckled," said Concord in the seat behind his dad.

"All set," said Faith in the seat behind Uncle Joe.

"Then we're ready to roll," Mr. Cunningham said with a smile. Today was the first full day of travel in the journey to Washington, D.C. After helping Chief Riggins capture the City Sign Bandit, they had followed the Capitol Christmas Tree truck about two hundred miles last night. They would have rather started the trip this morning, but they had to follow the tree truck no matter where or when it drove.

The journey had begun in Pine Tops, which was nestled in the upper reaches of the Pacific Northwest. From there, the truck drivers drove to a motel near the border of Washington and Idaho. Following a quick night's sleep and an early breakfast, the truck drivers were back in the truck. And the Cunninghams were back in their van.

"Let's see," said Uncle Joe as he looked at a map, "we went a couple hundred miles last night. So that's two hundred miles down, and about two-and-a-half-thousand to go."

Concord's eyes opened wide as he considered the distance. Then he looked down at the floor of the van to survey their supplies.

Concord knew that a successful road trip needed at least two things: snacks and activities. And this group had plenty of both. Concord and his dad had brought a large grocery bag full of snacks. Faith and Uncle Joe had brought a large cooler of drinks. And all of them had brought activities that they thought would be fun to do in the van.

"There it goes," Uncle Joe said as he pointed at the Capitol Christmas Tree truck. It was pulling onto the highway.

"And here we go," Mr. Cunningham added, putting the van in gear and following.

"Did you talk to the truck drivers about today's route?" Uncle Joe asked Mr. Cunningham.

"Sure did," he replied as the van accelerated. "They said they're going to follow this highway for a few miles to Interstate 90. Then they'll get on the interstate and head east. I guess one of the drivers has a favorite gas station along the interstate a few hours from here. They're going to stop there to fill up."

Faith asked, "Did the truck drivers think it was strange that we'd be following them all the way to Washington, D.C.?"

"Not at all," Mr. Cunningham answered. "They know that the media always cover this kind of thing. In fact, they said we'll probably run into quite a few other reporters covering the story along the way."

A few miles down the road, Concord decided that the best way to start the day was to open the cooler and have some of his favorite drink: chocolate milk. He opened the tall, slender milk carton and poured some chocolate milk into a paper cup. Then he sat back, took a sip, and enjoyed the scenery. As the miles went by, Concord took more and more sips, and poured more and more cups. Before he knew it, the carton was empty!

"Uh-oh," Concord murmured.

"What is it?" Faith asked.

"Well, there's a situation with the chocolate milk," Concord said.

"What kind of situation?" Faith asked.

Concord held up the open carton and turned it upside-down. "It's gone."

Faith grinned. "Let me guess," she said, "it was last seen going past your lips and hasn't been heard from since?"

"You guessed it," he said with a chuckle.

"Don't worry Concord," Faith said, "We can find more."

But finding more chocolate milk would be the least of Concord's milk problems. The entire carton of milk was working its way through his system. And about two hours later, Concord was anxious to find a rest stop.

"Dad, do you think we're getting close to that gas station yet?" Concord asked as his leg twitched.

Mr. Cunningham looked at his watch. "We've been on the road for a few hours," he said as he scratched his cheek. "It probably isn't too far away."

Faith turned toward Concord and observed his twitching leg. "Do you have another, uh, chocolate milk situation?" she asked.

"You guessed it," Concord replied. Then he closed his eyes and waited.

A few minutes later, Faith nudged Concord. She pointed at the Capitol Christmas Tree truck, which was exiting the interstate. They were at the base of a mountain range, and this was the last exit before the long climb to the summit. The gas station was the only building in sight, and it was called "Last Chance Gas."

"Whew, just in time," Concord said with relief.

As soon as Mr. Cunningham parked the van, Concord unbuckled his seatbelt, burst out of the van, and ran into the small old building.

"Excuse me," Concord quickly said to the cashier. "Do you have a restroom?"

The man wore a greasy shirt and a yellow baseball cap. "It's around back," he replied. "But, it's -- "

Before the cashier could finish, Concord dashed out the door and ran around to the back of the building. But instead of rushing through the restroom door, he suddenly stopped. The restroom was closed!

There was a slab of wet cement extending about ten feet in all directions from the restroom door. The new cement was roped off so no one would step in it until it dried.

"Sorry, kid," a construction worker said to Concord. The worker wore heavy black boots, brown pants, and a bright yellow vest. "No one gets in until the cement is dry." Then he looked down at the cement and shook his head. "Well, almost no one."

Concord took a closer look at the cement. There were two sets of footprints going right through the middle of it! One set belonged to a person, and the other belonged to a dog. Both sets of footprints started at the edge of the new slab of cement and went straight to the restroom door.

"I guess somebody couldn't wait to go," the worker said.

"I know the feeling," Concord said with a sigh.

Just then, Mr. Cunningham and Uncle Joe arrived. The truck drivers were a few steps behind them. They all shook their heads as they looked at the footprints.

"Do you know who did it?" Mr. Cunningham asked the construction worker.

"Not yet, but I will as soon as he comes out of there," the construction worker said.

"How did he sneak by you?" Uncle Joe asked.

"After I had finished smoothing the cement, I went back to my truck for a coffee break," the construction worker said. He pointed toward the far end of the parking lot, where the cement truck was now parked. "A few minutes later, I came back and saw the footprints going into the bathroom. I couldn't believe that somebody would do that!" Then he tapped his foot impatiently. "I know that whoever is in there will come out sooner or later, and I'm going to make him help me fix this!"

Mr. Cunningham knelt by the new cement and touched it. It was still wet. "Are you sure there isn't any other way out of the restroom?" he asked the construction worker.

The worker stood silent. He had never considered the possibility. "I'm not sure," he finally answered. "I didn't go in there before I started the project."

One of the drivers quickly went to get the cashier so they could ask him the same question. A moment later, the driver and the cashier came walking around the corner.

"Nope, there's no other way out of there," the cashier said as he arrived. "No windows, no skylights, nothing. And the wet cement is definitely too big of a patch for a person to jump across. Whoever is in there is stuck."

The group nodded in agreement.

"What I want to know is why somebody would take a dog into the bathroom," Uncle Joe said.

"Good question," agreed Mr. Cunningham.

"Maybe he didn't want to leave the dog outside in the

cold," the cashier replied.

"Maybe it was a guide dog for a blind person," the construction worker said.

"Or maybe he just didn't have a leash and was worried the dog would run away," the cashier added.

"I guess we can ask him about that when he comes out," Mr. Cunningham said.

They all stood silently for a moment.

"It sure is quiet in there," Mr. Cunningham observed. Then he turned to the construction worker. "How long have you been waiting for them to come out?"

The construction worker looked at his watch. "About an hour," he said.

"What?" Mr. Cunningham said with surprise. "He's been in there an hour? He must know that you're waiting for him. He's probably waiting for you to leave."

"No chance of that," the construction worker said. "I'll stay all day if I need to."

Concord suddenly made a dash for the parking lot. A minute later he was back with his backpack. He dropped it to the ground, pulled out his Bible, and started flipping pages.

The confused construction worker watched Concord. "What's he doing?" he asked.

"I think he's trying to help you," Mr. Cunningham said with a grin.

"With a Bible?" the construction worker asked.

Concord tapped a page and looked up. "I don't think you're going to catch the person who left those footprints, or his dog," Concord said. "I think they escaped."

"What?" the construction worker said with surprise. "How could reading the Bible make you think that?"

"It's because of Jeremiah 7:24," the Concordance said. "Let me read it to you and maybe you'll see what I mean."

How did the person and the dog escape from the restroom?

Read Jeremiah 7:24 for the clue that Concord gave the construction worker.

The solution to The Disappearing Dog Walker is on page 100.

4
THE
ICE FISH SHACK

"Welcome to the Ice Fish Shack," the waitress said with a smile. "What can I get for you today?" The Cunninghams scanned their menus. They were on a dinner break after traveling on the interstate all afternoon.

They had followed the Capitol Christmas Tree truck along Interstate 90 to this restaurant in a small Montana town. Concord hadn't paid attention to the name of the town, but he knew that it was somewhere between Bozeman and Billings.

Mr. Cunningham folded his menu with a sigh and looked up at the waitress. "What would you recommend?" he asked.

The waitress lowered her order pad and pencil. Then she bit her lower lip as she thought. She wore a green uniform covered with fish patches, and her hair was pulled into a ponytail. "Have you been here before?" she asked.

All the Cunninghams shook their heads.

"Well then it's an easy choice," she said with a grin. "You should order our famous Ice Fish Shack Special Catch Platter Splatter."

"I would order it, but don't think I can even say it," Mr. Cunningham joked.

The group chuckled.

"What exactly is it?" Uncle Joe asked.

"It's a delicious platter of fried fish caught by local ice fishermen," she said.

"Ice fishermen?" Faith repeated with curiosity. She'd never heard of ice fishing. "Do ice fishermen use ice cubes for bait?"

The waitress laughed. "No, no," she said. "They use fishing poles, bait, and fishing hooks just like everybody else. Ice fishing is when you go out on a frozen lake, cut a hole in the ice, and drop your fishing line in the hole. You see, the lake isn't frozen all the way to the bottom, and the fish are still alive under the ice."

Uncle Joe looked out the window. "Isn't it a little early in the winter for the lakes around here to be frozen?" he asked.

"It is early in the winter around here," the waitress agreed. "But winter comes earlier in the high mountains, and some of the lakes up there are already frozen. That's where our fishermen have been going this week."

"Are the fish still fresh by the time they get back to the restaurant?" Concord asked.

"Absolutely," the waitress answered. "The fishermen bring us fresh fish every day. And they always deliver the fish the same day the fish are caught. In fact, today's delivery is just arriving now. It doesn't get much fresher than that!"

Mr. Cunningham nodded. "Well, you've sold me," he said. "I'll take the Ice Fish Fatter Matter Splatter on a Platter. Wait, did I say that right?"

They all laughed. Mr. Cunningham looked up toward the ceiling and started mumbling words to himself as he tried to figure out the name of the meal.

Uncle Joe turned to Faith. "Maybe you could help your Uncle Bill," he said.

Faith nodded. "He'd like the Ice Fish Shack Special Catch Platter Splatter," she said.

"Thanks Faith," Mr. Cunningham said. "I'm not sure my stomach could have waited long enough for me to figure out how to say that," he joked.

The waitress then looked at Uncle Joe for his order. "I'll also take the Ice Fish Splatter Shack-," he stopped. "I'll take what he's having," he said as he pointed at Mr. Cunningham.

"I will, too," Concord said. He wasn't a big fish fan, but he was excited to try something new.

Faith was just about to order the same thing. Right before she opened her mouth, Concord asked the waitress a question. "By the way, what's the 'splatter' part of the meal?" he asked.

"Oh, the fish is smothered in our special spinach and liver sauce," the waitress answered.

The group sat silently for a moment.

"I'll take the cheeseburger and fries," Faith said.

"Okay," the waitress said with a nod. "That's three Ice Fish Shack Special Catch Platter Splatters and one cheeseburger and fries coming right up!"

The waitress collected their menus and hurried off to the kitchen.

A few minutes later, Concord watched the restaurant door open and saw a man wearing a long brown coat enter the restaurant.

The Cunninghams were sitting near the front of the restaurant, so they could easily hear the man as he began talking to the hostess near the front door.

"Hello," the man said. "I'm Dirk Wayne from the Billings Gazette, and I have a few questions for the owner."

Mr. Cunningham and Uncle Joe looked at each other. Because Mr. Wayne introduced himself as a reporter, they knew he must be working on a story.

The hostess went to the back of the restaurant and entered an office. A minute later she returned with a tall woman who had gray hair and wore a blue business suit.

"I'm Janelle West," the owner said. "How may I help you?"

"Mrs. West," Mr. Wayne began, "I've been covering a story about fish being stolen from the hatchery to the north of town. I've heard rumors that those stolen fish may be served as meals at this restaurant. Is that true?"

"That's ridiculous!" Mrs. West said with a scowl. "We hire fishermen to go up to the high mountain lakes to catch our fish. They bring us fresh fish every day."

"Every day?" Mr. Wayne asked.

"That's right," Mrs. West replied.

"Are there ever any days when the fishermen don't catch fish?" Mr. Wayne asked.

Mrs. West considered the question for a moment. "I can't remember that ever happening," she said.

"So your fishermen catch fish every time they go fishing," Mr. Wayne said. "Did you ever find it strange that your fishermen may just be the luckiest fishermen in the world?"

Mr. Cunningham turned to Uncle Joe. "This guy is good," he whispered. Uncle Joe nodded in agreement.

Mr. Wayne reached into his pocket and pulled out a picture. He showed it to Mrs. West. "This is a picture from one of the security cameras at the hatchery," he said. "It shows two men reaching over the hatchery fence with a long pole. There's a fishing net attached to the end of the pole. You can see that they're going to dip the net into the hatchery pools."

He handed the picture to Mrs. West. She studied it carefully. Then he pulled out another picture. "This one was taken a few seconds later," he explained. "You'll see that the net is now full of fish. The two men are clearly stealing fish from the hatchery."

Concord leaned toward his dad. "How can they just scoop the fish out of the water like that?" he asked. "Aren't the fish hard to catch?"

"The hatchery pools are loaded with fish," his father

explained. "You can easily scoop them out with a net. It's like dipping your spoon into a bowl of cereal. It's almost impossible to miss."

Mrs. West studied the second picture carefully. "These men are definitely stealing the fish," she agreed. "But I can't tell if they are my fishermen or not."

Mr. Wayne nodded. He knew that the pictures were not clear enough to identify people.

"I've got an idea," Mrs. West said. "The fishermen just unloaded today's delivery at the back of the restaurant. If we look at the fish, maybe we could tell if they're the fish from the hatchery."

"I thought of that, too," Mr. Wayne replied. "But I did some research and learned that the fish stolen from the hatchery are the same kind of fish found in the mountain lakes. In fact, many of the hatchery fish are released into those lakes. So I'm afraid that the lake fish and the hatchery fish are exactly alike, and we wouldn't learn anything by looking at today's delivery."

Concord stood up. "Dad, I need to run back to the van for a minute," he said.

Mr. Cunningham smiled. He knew what Concord was up to. "Go for it!" he said.

A few minutes later, Concord was back with his Bible. Mr. Cunningham noticed that Concord had his finger on a verse. That meant Concord was ready.

Mr. Cunningham stood up and walked over to Mr. Wayne and Mrs. West. "Hello," he said. "I'm sorry to interrupt. My name is Bill Cunningham. I was sitting at a table a few feet away, and I couldn't help overhearing the situation. I'd like you to meet my son, Concord."

Mr. Cunningham motioned for Concord to come over to the group. "Concord might be able to help you out," he said.

Mr. Wayne flipped to a new page in his reporter's notepad. "Were you a witness to the crime?" he asked.

"No," Concord answered.

"Did you see the fishermen up at a mountain lake?" Mr. Wayne asked.

"No," Concord answered again. "But I can help you figure out whether or not the fishermen actually got their fish from the lake."

"You can?" Mr. Wayne said with surprise. "How?"

"Do you know anyone who can do a close inspection of the fish?" Concord asked.

"Sure," Mr. Wayne answered. "I know a biologist who could inspect every millimeter of the fish with his magnifying equipment. But, as I said before, the fish at the hatchery are exactly like the fish in the lake. Inspecting them wouldn't help."

"Actually it would, according to this," Concord said as he tapped his Bible.

Mr. Wayne and Mrs. West looked at each other and laughed.

"Is this a joke?" Mr. Wayne asked. "We're not in church. How could the Bible help?"

"The Bible isn't just for church," Concord replied. Then he handed his Bible to Mr. Wayne. "Here, try reading Job 41:1. I think you'll realize how to tell if the fishermen are the thieves."

How will they know if the fishermen got their fish from the lake or from the hatchery?

Read Job 41:1 for the clue that Concord gave Mr. Wayne.

The solution to the Ice Fish Shack is on page 101.

5
THE
SUPER SPILL

"I'd say they're about as white as egg shells," Concord said as he looked toward the front of the van.

"Maybe they were that white a couple of minutes ago," Faith said. "But now they're as white as lightening!"

Concord and Uncle Joe nervously chuckled as they nodded in agreement. They were driving east on Interstate 90 through South Dakota. They had crossed the Missouri River a few minutes ago. As they did, a huge snow storm suddenly blew in from the south, and the weather almost instantly changed to blizzard-like conditions.

The snow wasn't sticking yet, but the roads were getting slick. As the van rolled down the interstate, it was surrounded by a swirl of white. But that wasn't the white that Concord and Faith had been describing. They were talking about Mr. Cunningham's knuckles, which were clinging to the steering wheel with an iron grip. And he wasn't the only one with tight hands. With each passing minute, Concord nervously squeezed his bag of potato chips a little bit tighter.

"Do you think the tree truck will pull over and wait for the worst of the storm to pass?" Mr. Cunningham asked. He could barely see the truck's tail lights through the blowing snow, even though the truck was just ahead of them.

"I'm not sure," Uncle Joe answered as the van suddenly rocked to the left. The high winds were pushing it all over the road. "They wouldn't get an argument from me, though."

"Me neither," Mr. Cunningham agreed.

"Me neither," Concord added just as another gust hit the van. The bag of chips rustled as Concord squeezed it again.

"I don't think the potato chips would mind pulling over either," Faith joked. "At least what's left of them."

Concord laughed as he looked down and realized what he'd been doing.

"Tell the potato chips they're in luck," Mr. Cunningham said. "It looks like the truck is slowing down. We're only going about thirty miles per hour now." Then he looked down at the dashboard. "Wait, make that twenty." And then, a moment later, "Now we're down to ten." And just a few seconds later, they came to a stop.

"I guess the drivers decided it was too dangerous to keep driving," Faith said.

"Actually, I don't think they stopped by choice," Mr. Cunningham replied.

"What do you mean?" Faith asked.

"They didn't pull over to the side of the road. We're still in the middle of it," Mr. Cunningham answered.

"Is it a traffic jam?" Concord asked.

Mr. Cunningham leaned his head against the side window to look down the road, but he couldn't see around the tree truck. "I can't tell what's going on," he said. "Maybe it's an accident. We could be stuck here for a while."

Uncle Joe let out a deep breath. "Well, maybe this would be a good time for a snack," he said.

Concord held out the chip bag. "How about some potato, uh, crumbs?"

023

They all laughed.

A few minutes later, a state trooper approached the van. He wore a black overcoat and a black hat with a round brim. Mr. Cunningham rolled down his window. "Hello, officer," he said.

"Good afternoon," the officer said with a slight nod. "We've got a crash up ahead, and I'm afraid no vehicles are getting through until we can get the mess cleaned up."

"Was anyone hurt?" Mr. Cunningham asked.

The officer grinned. "Nope, everyone's okay," he said. Then he shook his head. "It's just a huge mess."

"What happened?" Mr. Cunningham asked.

"A semi-truck and its two trailers somehow got knocked onto their sides," the officer explained. "It couldn't have happened to a worse truck."

"Why is that?" Mr. Cunningham asked.

"See for yourself," the officer said as he started walking away. "I've got to keep working my way down the line of cars."

Mr. Cunningham turned to Uncle Joe. Uncle Joe nodded. Mr. Cunningham nodded back. Then Uncle Joe took film out of one of the pockets of his tan vest and loaded it into his camera. Mr. Cunningham grabbed his reporter's notepad off the dashboard.

"Are you guys really going out into the storm?" Faith asked.

"You bet," Uncle Joe said. "Your uncle and I are supposed to report on everything that happens along the way to Washington, D.C., and from what the officer said, this could be an interesting scene."

Concord suddenly put on his hat and stuck his Bible in one of the large pockets on the front of his coat.

"You're going out there, too?" Faith asked.

"I just realized that I could be the only Scripture Sleuth around for miles," Concord replied. "And you never know when somebody will need answers."

Mr. Cunningham turned back toward Concord. "Good thinking," he said with a wink. Then he turned to Faith. "What do you say, Faith? Do you want to join our snow storm adventure?"

Faith bit her lower lip as she thought for a moment. Then she grabbed her mittens. "I guess it would be better than sitting here alone in the van," she said.

A moment later, the Cunninghams were out in the storm. As they made their way along the line of cars and trucks, the storm began to weaken. And by the time they made it to the crash scene, the snow had nearly stopped falling.

"All that snow and none of it even stuck," Uncle Joe said as he walked along the wet pavement.

"Yeah, I was hoping to throw a snowball or two," Concord said. Then he looked up and saw the crash scene. Just as the officer had described, a semi-truck with two trailers had been knocked on its side. The truck and the two trailers lay in the middle of the eastbound interstate, blocking all traffic.

The trailers had open tops. They had been covered with tarps, but the tarps on both trailers had been torn off in the crash, so the contents of the trailers spilled all along the right side of the interstate.

"I've never seen so many balls in my life!" Concord exclaimed.

"There must be thousands of them," Uncle Joe added. He raised his camera to his eye and began looking for the perfect angle for a picture. He finally decided that the best shot would be with the camera at ground level. He looked at the wet pavement, shrugged, and then laid down flat on his stomach. "Perfect," he said as he snapped a shot.

"I don't know how you could even count that many balls," Mr. Cunningham said as he stared at the scene.

The trailers had been loaded to their brims with white plastic balls. Though the balls had flown everywhere when the trailers crashed, most of them had rolled off the side of the road and into a large construction pit.

A man approached the stunned Cunninghams. "I'll bet that's the world record for the number of holes-in-one with one shot," the man joked.

Mr. Cunningham turned to the man, who was wearing a yellow construction cap and an orange coat. "Were you working in the pit when the truck crashed?" Mr. Cunningham asked as he whipped out his notepad.

"Nope," the man said. "When the storm rolled in, I decided to take a break," he said. "Before that, I had been digging the pit with that backhoe right over there." He pointed to a large machine with a scoop on the back end.

"So what's the pit for?" Uncle Joe asked.

"We're building a big drainage pond," he said.

"Is it almost done?" Mr. Cunningham asked.

The worker shook his head. "It needs to be quite a bit deeper," he answered. "We're behind schedule, too. I was supposed to finish digging last week so we could install the fence during the weekend."

Concord saw bundles of chain link fencing resting near the pit. As he looked closer at the scene, he saw a man sitting just off the road near the edge of the pit. The man had his face buried in his hands.

Concord gently nudged his dad. "Hey, dad," he said as he pointed toward the man. "Do you think that's the truck driver?" he asked. Mr. Cunningham nodded.

"Poor guy," the construction worker said. The group stood silent for a moment. "Well, the least I can do is offer to help him clean up the balls," the construction worker said. "My backhoe could scoop them up and into his trailers pretty quickly."

"That ought to brighten his day a little bit," Mr. Cunningham said. "We'll come with you. Maybe we can help, too."

The group approached the driver, who wore blue jeans and a heavy blue flannel jacket.

"Hello, buddy," the construction worker said. "We're here to help."

The driver looked up. "You are?" he asked.

"I operate that backhoe over there," the construction worker said as he pointed across the pit. "Once you get your truck back up on its wheels, I'd be happy to scoop all these balls into your trailers for you. I'll bet we could get it done in an hour."

The driver looked across the pit at the backhoe. "I appreciate the offer," he said. "Everyone's been so nice to me. A crane is on the way, and it will have my truck back on its wheels in a couple of hours. A mechanic stopped by and told me my truck would be okay to drive." Then he sighed. "But even with all this help, I still have a huge problem."

"What's that?" Mr. Cunningham asked.

"These balls are parts of toys," he explained. "They are supposed to be at a toy factory a few miles from here by five o'clock today. If they're late, the factory won't be able to assemble the toys by the shipping deadline, and I lose my pay for this job."

Concord looked at his watch and started doing some math in his head. "It's one o'clock now," he said. "If your truck is ready to go in two hours, and the balls are back in the trailers an hour or so after that, won't you still be able to make it?" Concord asked.

"If it were that simple, I probably would," the driver said. "But take a closer look at the balls. They aren't all the same size."

Sure enough, some balls were the size of baseballs and some balls were the size of golf balls. Concord walked forward a couple of steps, reached down, and picked up a ball of each size. He held them up to show the group.

"Why does it matter if they're different sizes?" Faith asked.

"Because one size goes in one trailer, and the other size goes in the other trailer," the driver said. "They can't be mixed together. That's part of my delivery contract."

Uncle Joe looked at the thousands of balls and his hand gently slapped his cheek in shock. Mr. Cunningham's jaw dropped. Faith's eyes bulged. And Concord's hand reached into his coat pocket.

"It would take us days to separate the two sizes of balls," Uncle Joe said.

The driver nodded.

"What if we asked all the people who are stuck in the line of cars behind the wreck to help us?" Faith asked.

"I doubt very many people would volunteer to help after being stuck for so long," Mr. Cunningham said.

"Well, I'd be happy to scoop the balls into the trailers, anyway," the construction worker said to the driver. "I'm sorry you're not going to make your deadline, but I've got to get the balls out of the pit so I can finish my job."

"I'm not so sure that he's going to miss his deadline," Concord said. He was still standing at the edge of the balls, holding his Bible in his hand.

"What do you mean?" the driver asked. "And why are you reading the Bible?"

"I'm not just reading it," Concord answered. "I'm using it. And I think it may have the answer to your problem."

"How could that be?" the construction worker asked.

"Let's just say that I'm glad the drainage pond project is behind schedule. Here, read Luke 22:31," The Concordance said. "Maybe you'll see what I mean."

What is Concord's solution to the problem?

Read Luke 22:31 for the clue Concord gave to the group.

The solution to the Super Spill is on page 102.

6
TASTE TEST TROUBLES

"Okay everybody, it's time to put your shoes back on," Mr. Cunningham announced. "It looks like we're stopping for the night." The van was following the tree truck as it exited Interstate 80. They were near Des Moines, Iowa.

Concord reached down to the floor and grabbed his shoes. At a rest stop earlier in the day, he had picked up a magazine with traveling tips. One of the tips it offered was to remove your shoes while taking long drives. Concord had tried it in the morning, and he loved it. By lunch time, Faith had taken hers off, too. And by the middle of the afternoon, Concord and Faith were enjoying it so much that Uncle Joe decided to try it, too. It only took one hour for Uncle Joe to become a believer in road trip foot freedom.

After exiting the interstate, the van followed the tree truck a few blocks down a busy street to a large hotel. Both vehicles parked in the lot. As Uncle Joe, Faith, and Concord all opened their doors, Concord noticed that his dad wasn't getting out of the van.

"Are you coming, Dad?" Concord asked.

"I'll be with you in a minute," Mr. Cunningham replied.

Uncle Joe glanced over at Mr. Cunningham and chuckled. "It looks like somebody else tried taking shoes off, too," he announced.

Concord leaned forward and looked at his dad's feet.

Sure enough, Mr. Cunningham had been driving in his socks.

"Whoa!" Concord exclaimed with a giggle. "I didn't think Dad would go for it, too!"

"Well," Mr. Cunningham said with a grin, "as a reporter, I always need to stay on top of the latest trends."

"Do you think you'll be writing a story about this trend?" Uncle Joe asked.

"Probably not," Mr. Cunningham said. Then he rubbed his chin and smirked. "But if I did, the headline would be 'Sock n'Roll.'"

They all laughed, and Mr. Cunningham laced up his shoes. A moment later, they were all on their way into the hotel. Concord hadn't bothered to wear his coat, and it only took a few steps for him to start shivering.

"Wow, this is the coldest it's been the whole trip," he said.

"The bank thermometer two blocks back said it was twenty degrees," Faith said. "And I was listening to a local radio station with my headphones a few miles back. The announcer said the high temperature in the region for the past week has only been twenty-nine degrees."

"No wonder my arms feel like icicles," Concord said as he gave himself a hug to warm up.

They walked through the front doors of the hotel. The lobby was rather large and had a beautiful hard wood floor. At the far right side of the lobby was a huge fireplace with a roaring fire. There were two couches, two chairs, and a large coffee table surrounding the fireplace. At the far left end of the lobby was the reception desk.

As Mr. Cunningham and Uncle Joe checked in, Faith and Concord decided to go warm up by the fire. They sat down across from a man wearing a black suit and a blue tie.

He was the only other person by the fire, and he was staring at two containers on the coffee table in front of him. He stared at the containers for so long that Concord began to get curious about them. They were shaped like water bottles, but they looked like they were made of metal.

"Excuse me, are those water bottles?" Concord finally asked.

The man nodded. "These are the fanciest water bottles you'll ever see," he said proudly.

Faith reached out and tapped one of the bottles to make sure it was metal. "Doesn't bottled water usually come in plastic bottles?" she asked.

"Yes, usually," the man said, "and sometimes it comes in glass bottles. But this bottled water is going to be different. It's a whole new brand that my company is going to begin selling. It's supposed to be much fancier than regular bottled water, so we put it in these shiny metal bottles. We also make a special collector's edition cork with black and gold stripes." He pointed at one of the bottles, which had the special cork. "And each bottle is filled all the way to the bottom of the cork, just as these were."

"Why do you do that?" Concord asked.

"It's mostly an advertising gimmick," the man explained. "People will think they're getting more for their money. Have you ever noticed that most water bottles aren't filled up to the very top when you buy them?"

"Come to think of it, you're right," Concord said with a nod.

Mr. Cunningham and Uncle Joe had finished getting registered and they arrived by the fire.

"Hey Dad," Concord said, "check out these water bottles. They're the fanciest ones ever made."

Mr. Cunningham and Uncle Joe bent down to take a

closer look.

"Hi, I'm Jeff Carson," said the man in the suit. He exchanged handshakes with Mr. Cunningham and Uncle Joe, who introduced themselves and their kids.

"Are you in the bottled water business?" Mr. Cunningham asked.

"I am until I get back to company headquarters," Mr. Carson said with a frown. "Then I'll probably be looking for a new job."

"Why is that?" Uncle Joe asked.

Mr. Carson took a deep breath and let it out slowly. He stared at the metal water bottles again. "These two bottles hold two different types of water," he explained. "One bottle has water filtered by a new filtering system that we call Fresh Zap. The other bottle has water filtered by another new filtering system that we call Quick Stir. I'm taking them back to headquarters for our executives to do an important taste test. They're going to decide which process is the one we'll use for this fancy new brand." He sighed. "My problem is that I lost track of which is which."

Concord noticed that the bottles didn't have labels. The only difference between them was that one bottle had a cork and one didn't. "Did you take the cork out of one of the bottles so you could tell them apart?" he asked.

Mr. Carson shook his head. "No, I think someone stole that cork last night," he answered. "I accidentally left the bottles in places where anyone could have taken the corks, or even the bottles." He blushed with embarrassment.

"Maybe we could help you figure it which bottle is which," Concord said.

Mr. Carson chuckled and shook his head. "I don't see how you possibly could," he replied. "I've been sitting here thinking about it for hours, and I don't think there's any possible way."

Mr. Cunningham rubbed his chin for a moment. "Why weren't the bottles labeled?" he asked. "Then there wouldn't be this problem."

"The executives didn't want to know which water came from which filter system," Mr. Carson explained. "They wanted it to be a true taste test. So when I was at the lab, I just placed a rubber band around the Fresh Zap bottle so I could tell the two bottles apart. However, the rubber band snapped when I was carrying the bottles from the lab to my car yesterday evening."

"Is that when you lost track of which was which?" Uncle Joe asked.

"Not quite," Mr. Carson replied. "When the rubber band snapped, I knew I had the Fresh Zap bottle in my left hand. I made sure that the Fresh Zap bottle was always in my left had and the Quick Stir bottle was always in my right hand. And when I was in the car, I made sure I put the Fresh Zap bottle in the front seat and the Quick Stir bottle in the back seat. I was going to drive straight from the lab to this hotel, and my plan was to get another rubber band as soon as I got here."

"When did the bottles get mixed up?" Concord asked.

"It all started when I pulled into the hotel parking lot," Mr. Carson explained. "I suddenly felt sick to my stomach. Very sick. I grabbed the Fresh Zap bottle off of the front seat and jumped out of the car. I hurried toward my hotel room, but I realized after a few steps that I had forgotten the Quick Stir bottle. So I ran back to the car."

"Are these bottles so valuable that you need to worry about them even when you're that sick?" Uncle Joe asked.

"These are the only two bottles that the lab produced with the two new systems," Mr. Carson said. "They are each worth quite a bit of money. Of course, when they are mass produced, they'll only cost pennies per bottle."

"So what happened next?" Concord asked.

"I set the Fresh Zap bottle on top of the car while I went through my pockets looking for my car keys. I found them, unlocked the car, and grabbed the Quick Stir bottle out of the back seat. By then, I was almost feeling like I was going to pass out. In fact, I felt so awful that I completely forgot to grab the Fresh Zap bottle off the top of my car when I went into the hotel!"

"Did you make it into the hotel okay?" asked Faith.

"Barely," Mr. Carson replied. "When I got to my hotel room door, I was getting very lightheaded. I knew I was only seconds away from passing out. I set the Quick Stir bottle on the hallway floor next to my door so I could use both of my hands to find my room key. I found it, rushed into my room, and fell onto the bed. I didn't wake up until the middle of the night. Unfortunately, I had left the Quick Stir bottle on the floor outside my door."

"So the Fresh Zap bottle was on top of your car and the Quick Stir bottle was in the hallway outside your hotel room door?" Mr. Cunningham asked.

"That's right," Mr. Carson replied.

"Then what happened?" Uncle Joe asked.

"When I woke up in the middle of the night, I still felt sick. But I realized where I had left the two bottles. I knew I had to get them because they were so valuable. So, I mustered all the strength I could. I grabbed the Quick Stir bottle off the floor outside my room. Then I went outside and grabbed the Fresh Zap bottle off the roof of my car."

"So they were both still there," Uncle Joe said. "I guess you lucked out."

"Not exactly," Mr. Carson said. "I did have both bottles.

But, because I was still sick, I forgot to use my system to keep them straight. I came back into my room, set both bottles on the bathroom counter, and I fell back into bed. When I woke up late this morning I felt much better, but I realized that I had no idea which bottle was which."

"Is there any chance you can go back to the lab and ask them to figure it out?" Mr. Cunningham asked.

"Not without paying them a lot of money," Mr. Carson said. While he explained how his company executives would not be too happy about that, Concord hurried out to the van, brought in his backpack, and pulled out his Bible.

After a minute of page flipping, he stopped. Then he tapped on a verse. "Of course!" he said excitedly.

Mr. Cunningham grinned at Concord. Then he turned back to Mr. Carson. "I think my son might know which bottle is which," he said.

Mr. Carson's forehead tightened in confusion. "What do you mean?" he asked.

Mr. Cunningham nodded at Concord. Concord nodded back. "The answer is right here in Job 37:10," The Concordance announced to the group.

"That talks about my water bottles?" Mr. Carson asked.

"Not exactly," Concord replied.

Mr. Cunningham leaned forward and rested his elbows on his knees. "Concord has learned that after you read the Bible, you must apply it to your situation," Mr. Cunningham explained. Then he turned to Concord. "So, Concord, which bottle is which?"

"The bottle without the cork is the Fresh Zap bottle," Concord answered.

"You'd better hand me that Bible," Mr. Carson said. "I've got to see this for myself."

How did Concord know that the bottle without the cork was the Fresh Zap bottle?

Read Job 37:10 for the clue that Concord gave Mr. Carson.

The answer to Taste Test Troubles is on page 103.

7
LAMP LOVE

"Okay, we'll see you soon!" Mr. Cunningham said into his cell phone. Then he pressed a button to end the call, and turned to the group. "Aunt Nancy was sure surprised to hear from me."

"Is she ready for company?" Uncle Joe asked.

"She must be," Mr. Cunningham said. "She wants us to come to her house right away."

Aunt Nancy lived in eastern Illinois, which was where the tree truck had stopped for the night. The Cunninghams were sitting in a fast food restaurant and had just finished dinner. They were excited to visit Aunt Nancy. So, they quickly left the restaurant, jumped into the van, and headed north out of town.

"Is it very far?" Concord asked, trying to decide whether or not he should take off his shoes.

"Her house is a few miles north of town," Mr. Cunningham answered. "It's not a long drive."

Faith looked out the window at the dark countryside. "Will it be hard to find her house in the dark?" she asked.

Mr. Cunningham and Uncle Joe looked at each other. After a brief pause, they both laughed.

Faith raised an eyebrow in confusion. "I didn't realize it was such a funny question," she said.

"Normally it wouldn't be, Faith," Uncle Joe said. "But Aunt Nancy is a lamp collector."

"What does she do with them?" Faith asked.

"Let's just say that she's never met a lamp she didn't like to use," Uncle Joe answered with a chuckle.

After weaving through farmland on a series of country roads, they arrived at Aunt Nancy's house. It was a large, two-story home with many windows. All the windows had their curtains open, and there seemed to be two or three lamps shining in each one. The house was so bright that it almost seemed to be on fire.

"So, Concord, what do you think?" Mr. Cunningham asked as he turned off the engine.

Concord stared at the glowing house for a moment. "It's spectacular," he said. His eyes enjoyed the warm lamp light on the dark winter evening. Then he grinned. "If I was a moth, this is where I'd want to be on summer nights."

"You and about a million of your closest friends," Faith joked.

"You might change your mind once you found out that Aunt Nancy has four or five gigantic bug zappers outside her house," Mr. Cunningham said. He suddenly turned around and gave Concord a quick poke in the stomach. "Zap!"

Concord let out a squeal, and the rest of the Cunninghams laughed as they got out of the van. A moment later, they were ringing the doorbell. Concord heard footsteps approach, and then the door opened.

"Hello, all!" Aunt Nancy said excitedly. She was eighty years old, but she was very lively. She had short gray hair and she wore a blue dress. She was also wearing her coat and holding her purse.

After they all exchanged hugs, Mr. Cunningham asked the obvious question. "Aunt Nancy, are you going somewhere?"

"Oh, yes. We all are!" she cried out. "I just heard that the old church in the next county is auctioning its original furniture tomorrow morning. They're having a preview of all the items tonight, and I would just love to see if they'll be auctioning any lamps. I thought you all might be interested in taking a little drive with me."

The Cunninghams knew how much Aunt Nancy liked to find antique lamps, so they quickly agreed.

They decided to take the Cunninghams' van. Aunt Nancy climbed into the front passenger seat, and Uncle Joe sat in the back with Concord and Faith.

After driving straight north for about fifteen minutes, Aunt Nancy pointed toward a road coming up on the left. "That's our turn," she said. "It's called Wildwood Lane. It goes through the woods and comes out near the church. Now don't miss the turn, Bill, unless you want to take the long way around. It would only take us a couple of extra hours," she said with a laugh.

"The shorter the better," Mr. Cunningham said as he turned the steering wheel. Wildwood Lane was dark and narrow, and there was very little traffic. As the miles passed, Concord listened to the conversation and looked out the window. The road took them through thicker and thicker woods. Finally, just before the end of the road, trees of all sizes were growing right along the edge of the road. Concord felt like the van was driving through a tunnel.

At the end of Wildwood Lane, they turned north and only had to drive two more minutes to get to the church. As soon as Mr. Cunningham parked the van, Uncle Joe hopped out and opened the front passenger door for Aunt Nancy.

"Thank you, Joe," she said with a big smile. She grabbed Uncle Joe's arm and slowly climbed out. Uncle Joe

CONCORD CUNNINGHAM COAST TO COAST: THE Scripture Sleuth 4

closed the door behind her, and they all began to walk through the parking lot toward the old country church.

After a few steps, Aunt Nancy stopped. The smile on her face disappeared.

"What's wrong, Aunt Nancy?" Uncle Joe asked.

"It looks like Mr. Clark is here," she said with a scowl.

"Who's he?" Mr. Cunningham asked.

"There are two people in this area who collect antique lamps," she explained. "I am one, and Mr. Clark is the other. And when the lamps are auctioned, only one of us tries to win them honestly."

"What do you mean?" Concord asked.

"Mr. Clark always tries to trick me out of bidding for the lamps," she explained. "An hour before the last auction, he called to tell me that the auction was cancelled. I found out that he was lying. He was trying to make me miss the auction so I wouldn't be able to bid on the lamps! At the auction before that, right before an antique lamp was up for bid, he spilled coffee on my dress. He did it on purpose. He thought I would miss the auction when I went to clean my dress."

"Did you?" Faith asked.

Aunt Nancy grinned. "I stayed in my seat until that lamp had been auctioned," she said proudly. "And by the end of it, the coffee had gone through my dress, dripped down my stockings, and gone right into my shoes!" Aunt Nancy laughed at the memory, and the Cunninghams burst out laughing along with her.

After everyone had calmed down, Uncle Joe had a question. "How do you know Mr. Clark is here tonight?" he asked. The group was walking again.

"That's his truck," Aunt Nancy said as she pointed at a blue, compact-sized pickup that they were walking past.

A minute later they were inside the church, and Aunt Nancy had found what she was seeking. It was a beautiful white ceramic lamp decorated with golden roses. It also had a fancy shade. "It's absolutely breathtaking!" Aunt Nancy said with delight. "And it must be at least one hundred years old!"

"I'd say one hundred and twenty," said a man standing behind them.

Aunt Nancy turned toward the voice. "Good evening, Mr. Clark," she said with a nod. Mr. Clark wore a yellow collared shirt and black pants. Aunt Nancy quickly introduced the group. "These are my nephews, Bill and Joe Cunningham. And their children, Concord and Faith."

"Nice to meet you all," he said with a quick wave of his left hand. Before anyone could respond, he turned back to Aunt Nancy. "Well, don't get too excited about this lamp. It's going to be all mine."

Aunt Nancy smiled politely. "You mean it'll be yours if you're the winning bidder," she said. "You still need to beat me in the auction."

"We'll see about that," he said with a smirk. Then he turned and walked toward the other side of the church.

Concord turned toward his dad. "What did Mr. Clark mean by that, Dad?" he asked.

Mr. Cunningham thought for a moment. "I'm not sure," he said. "But it sounds like he's up to something again." Then Mr. Cunningham pulled the group into a close huddle. "Keep your eyes and ears open while we're here," Mr. Cunningham whispered. "Let's see what we can find out."

"Right," Concord said, and he gave his dad a thumbs-up. Uncle Joe and Faith also gave a thumbs-up sign, and Aunt Nancy nodded.

The group split up and observed different people and different parts of the church. About fifteen minutes later, they were ready to leave. Rather than comparing notes in the church, they decided to talk in the van.

After everyone was seated, Mr. Cunningham flipped open his reporter's notepad. "I'll start," he said as he looked at his notes. "I talked to the auction organizer. He said that Mr. Clark asked him if they could auction the antique lamp as the first item tomorrow morning. The organizer said he agreed to do it. So, the lamp will be auctioned right when the auction starts at eight o'clock in the morning."

"That is unusual," Aunt Nancy said. "At auctions like this, they usually don't get to the good stuff until later in the auction. In fact, the first items are usually small and not very interesting. That's why I usually show up a little bit late."

"Does Mr. Clark know you usually arrive late?" Mr. Cunningham asked.

"Oh, yes," she replied. "But he's the same way. Of course, I suppose he won't be late tomorrow." Then Aunt Nancy made a fist and tapped her knee. "He certainly is sneaky! I'll make sure that I'm here on time tomorrow."

The group sat quietly for a moment.

Uncle Joe broke the silence. "I found out something, too," he said. "Did any of you see the doorway near the back of the church's stage? It had a curtain instead of a door."

Faith nodded. "That doorway also had a sign that said there were more items for sale behind the curtain, right?" she asked.

"Right," Uncle Joe said. "I went into the room to look around. I was standing by the doorway curtain when Mr.

Clark and his wife started talking on the other side of it."

"His wife was here, too?" Mr. Cunningham asked.

"Oh, yes," said Aunt Nancy. "I saw her across the room. She usually doesn't come to the auctions, but she always comes to these previews to tell her husband which items she'd like him to buy."

"I know eavesdropping is wrong," Uncle Joe said, "but they were talking loud enough for me to hear without even trying. It was hard to ignore."

"What did they say?" Aunt Nancy asked.

"I heard Mrs. Clark ask her husband about you, Aunt Nancy. Mr. Clark said that you had seen the lamp, but he told his wife not to worry. He said his plan would work and the lamp would be theirs. Then she asked Mr. Clark if he had what he needed for the plan. He said it was in the back of his truck. He also said no one would ever know that he was the one who did it. Then they decided to leave."

Concord looked out the van window and across the parking lot to where Mr. Clark's truck had been parked. Sure enough, it was gone. "Too bad the truck isn't still here," he said. "We could look in the back."

"No problem," Faith said with a smile. "I looked in the back of the truck when we walked by it earlier."

Concord raised his hand and gave Faith a high-five. "What was in there?" he asked.

"An open toolbox, and nothing else," Faith said. Then she closed her eyes. "The toolbox was divided into two parts. On the left side were many different sizes of screwdrivers. On the right side were a hammer and a saw." Then she opened her eyes. "And that's all there was."

Concord thought for a moment. Then he reached down to the floor for his backpack and pulled out his Bible.

"Do you think he's going to do something to Aunt Nancy's car tonight?" wondered Uncle Joe.

"I keep it locked in the garage," Aunt Nancy said. She scratched her cheek as she thought for a moment. "Mr. Clark may try to cheat in auctions, but I'd be surprised if he would actually try to break into my garage."

The van was silent, except for the rustling pages of Concord's Bible. Finally, Concord looked up. "I've got it!" he said excitedly.

Aunt Nancy gave Concord a surprised look. "You do?" she asked.

Concord tapped his Bible. "It's right here in 2 Kings 6:4," The Concordance said. "Mr. Clark is only going to use one of those tools, and I know where."

What is Mr. Clark's plan to stop Aunt Nancy from winning the antique lamp?

Read 2 Kings 6:4 for the clue that Concord gave Aunt Nancy.

The solution to "Lamp Love" is on page 104.

8
THE GREAT
TURTLE RACE

"It's only 11:15. Are the tree truck drivers ready for lunch already?" Uncle Joe asked. The tree truck's turn signal had just begun blinking, and the truck was slowing down to exit the interstate. The truck and van were rolling along Interstate 70 in Indiana.

"Either they're ready for an early lunch, or they're interested in the Great Turtle Race," Mr. Cunningham answered.

"The what?" Faith asked.

"I saw a sign along the road a little while ago," Mr. Cunningham explained. "It said that the Great Turtle Race was today at the local fairgrounds."

"I didn't know that turtles raced," Faith said. "Aren't they too slow?"

"I suppose that if they're all slow, it could be a pretty close race," Mr. Cunningham said with a slight shrug.

The tree truck and the van exited the interstate. Turn after turn, the tree truck followed the signs to the Great Turtle Race, and the van followed the truck. Finally, the two vehicles pulled into the parking lot at the county fairgrounds.

"Either there's a restaurant with a really good lunch menu here, or we've got a couple of turtle racing fans driving the tree truck," Mr. Cunningham said with a chuckle.

He parked next to the driver's side of the tree truck.

One of the truck drivers, Max, quickly opened the driver's side door and jumped out. Max always wore black jeans and a blue baseball cap. He did most of the driving, and he was about ten years younger than the other driver, Archie. Archie was sixty years old. He had a gray beard, and he always wore a red plaid jacket.

Max and Archie were very nice to the Cunninghams. They always tried to let Mr. Cunningham know what time they planned on leaving places. And the drivers always tried to find parking spots with nice backgrounds so Uncle Joe could get scenic pictures of the tree on the way to Washington, D.C.

After Max jumped out of the truck, the Cunninghams watched him reach behind the driver's seat and pull out a cage.

"Is that what I think it is?" Concord asked.

Uncle Joe sucked in a deep breath with surprise. "It sure is," he said excitedly. "Max has a turtle!"

"He's so cute!" Faith said as she leaned forward to see better.

The turtle was green, and its shell was about the size of a cereal bowl.

"I can't believe it," Mr. Cunningham said. "Max actually brought a turtle on this trip. How has he kept that a secret?"

Max took a few steps toward the van. Uncle Joe rolled down his window as Max approached. "Hi Max," Uncle Joe said. "Who's your friend?"

"This is Max Jr.," Max said with a grin. "We're going to make a short stop here. I saw the Great Turtle Race sign on the interstate and thought Max Jr. might enjoy stretching his legs. He's been in this cage for quite a while. If it won't take much time, I'd like to see if we can get him in the race."

"Has he been in the cage all the way from Pine Tops?" Mr. Cunningham asked.

"Almost," Max said. "I let him out of the cage on the first day of our trip. But there was an incident with Archie's turkey sandwich. Max Jr. was on the back of my seat when he saw Archie's sandwich on the cooler between Archie and me. Max Jr. managed to sneak down there and eat a good chunk of the sandwich before Archie noticed. Archie didn't like that too much," Max shrugged. "So, Max Jr. has been in his cage since then."

"Does he travel okay?" Mr. Cunningham asked.

"Yep," Max replied. "As far as he knows, the truck is his home. I take him with me on all my trips. Most hotels don't allow pets, but they don't seem to care about turtles."

Max looked across the parking lot toward the main building on the fairgrounds. "The sign says that the race starts in about thirty minutes. I think I'll go see if I can register Max Jr."

"He's a racing turtle?" asked Faith.

"Not really," Max said. "I've entered him in a few races, but he never wins. He enjoys it, though, because he gets to see other turtles."

Max gave a quick wave to the group, turned, and began walking toward the building.

"Does anybody feel like going in and cheering for Max Jr.?" asked Mr. Cunningham.

"Count me in!" Concord said excitedly as he unbuckled his seatbelt.

"Me, too!" Faith said, unbuckling just as fast as Concord.

"Sounds fun," Uncle Joe said. Then he grabbed his camera. "I'd better bring this in case it's a photo finish!"

The Cunninghams all laughed as they opened their van doors.

A few moments later they entered the building. It was a large open space with about two hundred people walking around. There was a racetrack in the middle. The racetrack had twenty straight lanes, which were painted on connected sheets of plywood. The track was about twenty feet long.

On the right end of the building was a large turtle pen with a short fence. Inside the pen were about fifteen turtles, lots of lettuce scraps, and a man wearing glasses and a red vest. He seemed to be in charge of the turtles.

On the other end of the building was the registration table. The Cunninghams saw Max doing some paperwork there, so they worked their way over to the table. They arrived just as Max handed his paperwork to a person behind the table.

"So is Max Jr. entered in the race?" Mr. Cunningham asked.

Max nodded. "He's all set," he said.

"What happens now?" asked Uncle Joe.

"It's social hour!" Max replied. "We need to put Max in the turtle pen so he can visit the other turtles. C'mon!" Max hurried over to the turtle pen and the Cunninghams followed. Max stood at the fence surrounding the turtle pen and caught the attention of the turtle wrangler. The wrangler carefully walked across the pen to Max and Max Jr.

"Hello, little fella," the turtle wrangler said as he gently stroked Max Jr.'s shell. Then the wrangler pulled a turtle treat out of his vest pocket and fed it to Max Jr. "Are you here to join us?"

"He sure is," Max said. "This is Max Jr."

"Hi Max Jr.," the wrangler said. "I'm Mr. Kelly." He pulled a notepad and pencil out of his other vest pocket and wrote down Max Jr.'s name. "Any special instructions?" he asked Max.

"Nope," Max said. "He should be fine."

"Okay," Mr. Kelly said as he scribbled something down. Then he stuck the notepad back into his vest pocket. "I'll be right back," he said. He carefully walked across the turtle pen to a small table. He picked up a cup of paint and a small paintbrush, and then he walked back. "I'm going to paint an 'M' on Max Jr.'s shell so everyone can identify him in the race. A lot of these turtles look alike, so this helps us keep them straight. The paint will wash right off after the race."

Max nodded and Mr. Kelly quickly painted the "M" on Max Jr.'s shell. Faith looked at the other turtles. They all had letters painted on their backs, except for one. Instead of a painted letter, he wore a bright yellow turtle sweater. In the middle of the sweater was a big letter "C."

"Why does that turtle have a sweater?" Faith asked Mr. Kelly. "Does he get cold?"

"No, that's Turbo," Mr. Kelly answered with a sigh. He seemed to become frustrated just looking at Turbo.

"Shouldn't Turbo have a 'T' on his sweater instead of a 'C?'" Faith asked.

"The 'C' stands for champion," Mr. Kelly explained. "Turbo won last year's race, and that sweater was the prize. He gets the honor of wearing it in this year's race, too." Mr. Kelly shook his head with disgust. "That turtle has won the race for the last five years in a row!"

"It sounds like you were rooting for a different turtle," Mr. Cunningham said.

Mr. Kelly pointed to a turtle in the middle of the pen

with a letter "D" painted on its shell. "That's Dudley," Mr. Kelly said. "He's mine. He has come in second the last three years in a row."

"Maybe this will be the year he finally beats Turbo," Uncle Joe suggested.

"Could be," Mr. Kelly said with a small grin.

The group said goodbye to Mr. Kelly and Max Jr., and they all went over to the racetrack. As race time drew near, an announcer stood in the middle of the racetrack and began introducing the turtles. The announcer was a large man with a leather coat and a deep voice.

As each turtle's name was announced, Mr. Kelley brought that turtle from the turtle pen to the racetrack. Then Mr. Kelley handed the turtle to its owner and gave the turtle a turtle treat. The owner would then step up to the microphone and tell the crowd a little bit about the turtle.

Since Turbo was the champion of last year's race, he was introduced last.

"Ladies and gentlemen," the announcer said through the speakers, "it's time to bring out last year's champion. Get ready. Get set. Here's Turbo!"

The crowd applauded. A few seconds later, Mr. Kelly made his way through the crowd to the center of the race-track and handed Turbo to his owner, Mrs. Parker. She had long red hair and wore a blue denim dress.

Mr. Kelley pulled a turtle snack out of his vest pocket and fed it to Turbo. Since all the turtles were now at the racetrack, Mr. Kelly took a few steps to the right and stood next to his turtle, Dudley.

Mrs. Parker said a few things about Turbo, and then it was finally race time.

"Turtles on your marks!" the announcer shouted through the speakers. The turtles were all lined up. Each turtle was in a lane, and there was a board stretched across the starting line. "Get set! Go!"

The board was removed, and the turtles were off and racing. At least some of them. About half of the turtles just stood at the starting line and looked around. Meanwhile, all of the turtle owners were waiting at the end of the race-track. They were doing whatever they could to get their turtles to race to the finish line. Some owners dangled shiny objects. Some held out food. And some just made funny noises with their lips.

"Do you think Max's plan will work?" Concord asked his dad.

"It looks like it's working already," Mr. Cunningham said with a grin. There at the end of Max Jr.'s lane was Archie, who was eating a turkey sandwich. Max must have seen the sandwich because he was leading the race!

But about halfway through the race, Dudley passed him. As Dudley got closer and closer to the finish line, Concord realized that Max Jr. wasn't going to catch up. Concord also realized something else. "Wait a minute," Concord said as he scanned the racetrack. "Where's Turbo?"

"He's back at the start," Faith answered. "He hasn't even moved."

About a minute later, Dudley crossed the finish line and Mr. Kelly picked him up with a huge smile. Mr. Kelly lifted Dudley high above his head and the crowd cheered. But a few seconds later, all the cheering stopped.

"Who did this?" Mrs. Parker cried. She was holding Turbo with one hand and using her other hand to lift up the edge of his sweater. "This isn't my Turbo. It's a different turtle!" she shouted as she peeked under his sweater.

Everyone in the building went silent and stared at Turbo

and Mrs. Parker.

"Mrs. Parker," the announcer said over the speakers, "are you certain that the turtle you're holding is not Turbo?"

"I'm positive," she said frantically. "Turbo has a small scar on his shell, right above his front right leg. This turtle doesn't have the scar. This is definitely a different turtle. And that means that Turbo has been turtlenapped!"

The crowd gasped. Everyone began looking around the room for suspects. It didn't take long for Mrs. Parker to point her finger.

"I know who it is!" Mrs. Parker shouted. The crowd became silent. "Mr. Kelley was this year's turtle wrangler. He was watching the turtles the whole time. He must have done it!"

Mr. Kelley raised his eyebrows in surprise. "Me?" he said. He swallowed nervously. "There were always people around the turtle pen. I wouldn't have had the chance to switch the turtles without being seen."

Faith nudged Concord. "Do you think Mr. Kelly did it?" she asked quietly.

"I'm not sure," Concord whispered. Then he scratched his chin. "Could you do me a favor?" he asked.

"Say no more," Faith replied with a grin. "I'll be right back." She quickly walked to the door and left the building. Meanwhile, Concord continued listening.

"Did anyone see anything that might help us figure this out?" the announcer asked the crowd.

A man from the back of the crowd raised his hand. "I saw Mr. Kelly carrying Turbo in the hallway by the back-door," he said. "It was right before Turbo's introduction."

"I saw him there with Turbo, too," a woman called out from the other side of the crowd.

"Well of course I was carrying Turbo around," Mr. Kelley

said. "It was my job to carry each turtle to the racetrack."

"But why did you have Turbo in the hallway by the back door?" Mrs. Parker asked.

Mr. Kelly swallowed nervously. Everyone was staring at him. "Well, I had to catch him," he said.

"What do you mean?" Mrs. Parker asked.

"Turbo had escaped from the turtle pen," Mr. Kelly said. He took a deep breath and let it out slowly. "Let me explain. While Turbo was in the turtle pen, it seemed to me that he wasn't feeling too well. He seemed like he was looking for something soft to rest on."

"He does like to rest on pillows at home," Mrs. Parker agreed.

"So, I took off my vest, folded it up, and let him lay down on it," Mr. Kelly explained. "While he rested there, I left the turtle pen to go get a drink at the water fountain. As I was walking back to the turtle pen, something on the floor caught my eye. It was Turbo and his bright yellow sweater. He had escaped! He was walking down the hallway toward the back door. I ran over there and picked him up. As I did, I noticed that he had managed to get part of his sweater dirty. He must have walked through some dirt or some spilled food or something like that. So, since there is a bathroom in that hallway, I took him in there to clean off his sweater. I knew that Mrs. Parker would want Turbo to look nice when he was introduced."

Mrs. Parker nodded. "I appreciate that," she said.

"I took Turbo's sweater off and quickly used a moist paper towel to clean it," Mr. Kelly said. "Then I put it back on him. Just as I was carrying Turbo back down the hallway, I heard his name announced on the speakers. So, I brought him straight to the racetrack to be introduced."

Faith had returned. She tapped Concord on the shoulder.

CONCORD CUNNINGHAM COAST TO COAST: THE *Scripture Sleuth 4*

"Here you go, Concord," she said. She handed him his Bible.

"Just in time," Concord said. He immediately opened it and began flipping pages.

"The only thing I can think of is that somebody else must have switched the turtles when I was at the water fountain," Mr. Kelly said. "I guess I didn't know Turbo well enough to tell the difference."

Mrs. Parker shrugged. She wasn't sure what to think. The crowd began mumbling quietly.

"Does anyone else have some information that might help?" the announcer asked.

Concord looked up at his dad and nodded. Mr. Cunningham nodded back. Then Concord raised his hand and stepped forward. "I do," he said. The crowd watched him as he opened his Bible. "Mr. Kelly's story can't be true," he said.

"And why not?" the announcer asked.

"Because of Mark 13:16," The Concordance said.

The announcer didn't know what to think of Concord's reply. Finally, he said, "Why don't you come over to the microphone and read that for us."

Concord did. When Mr. Kelly heard the verse, he knew that he had been caught in his lies.

How did Concord know that Mr. Kelly's story wasn't true?

Read Mark 13:16 for the clue that Concord gave the crowd.

The solution to The Great Turtle Race is on page 105.

9
BREAKDOWN
BLUES

Concord's eyes slowly opened. He lifted his head and looked out the van window. He had fallen asleep as the van rolled down Interstate 70 in eastern Ohio.

Everything looked blurry, so he rubbed his eyes. It didn't help. Then he blinked about ten times, but that didn't help. He finally decided that his eyes were fine, so there must be a problem with the window. He pressed his hand to the glass and rubbed in a circle. That still didn't help. He turned toward Faith and looked out her window. But the countryside still looked blurry.

"Is it foggy out?" Concord asked with a yawn.

"Nope," said Faith. "It's the tree truck. It's smoking."

"It's smoking?" Concord asked. He was still half-asleep, and the image of a huge cigar sticking out of the front of the large semi popped into his groggy head. Then his mind snapped back to life, and he suddenly straightened up in his seat. "The tree truck is smoking?" he repeated with panic. "Is the tree on fire?"

"No, no," said Mr. Cunningham. "The tree is fine. There's something wrong with the truck's engine."

"Are the drivers pulling over?" Concord asked.

"Not yet," Uncle Joe said. He was holding his camera up to his eye. It clicked twice. "Perfect," he said. "I'm sure the paper will want a picture of this."

"We're guessing that the drivers are trying to get to the little town just ahead," Mr. Cunningham said. "Hopefully there will be a mechanic there."

About a minute later, the semi exited the interstate and turned onto the small town's main road. After driving a few blocks, the truck came to a jerky stop in front of a repair shop. The van parked right behind the truck. Max and Archie climbed down from their seats and began walking toward the shop.

"Should we go into the repair shop, too?" Uncle Joe asked.

"Absolutely," Mr. Cunningham said as he grabbed his reporter's notepad. "I'd like to know how long the repair is going to take. And if this is something serious, I should probably get the story back to the Ponderosa Press right away."

Concord's legs were ready for a stretch, so he decided to go in as well. Faith wasn't too excited about visiting a repair shop, so she stayed in the van and read her book.

The repair shop wasn't big, but its walls were tall, which allowed it to hold large vehicles. The shop had one service bay. The service bay's door was open, and inside was a large motor home. The motor home was so long that the back part of it stuck out of the shop and into the parking lot. At the right end of the building was a small office area with a lower roof.

"It looks like the shop only has room for one vehicle at a time," Mr. Cunningham said as they walked toward the office.

"Hopefully they're just about done with the motor home," Uncle Joe added.

The Cunninghams walked through the office door and found Max and Archie standing in front of the service counter. There was no one behind it.

"Nobody home?" Mr. Cunningham asked.

Archie shook his head. "We're going to take a look around," he said. He and Max walked across the office to a door that led directly into the repair area. They opened it and went through. The Cunninghams followed.

"Hello?" Archie called out.

"In here!" a voice replied from inside the motor home. "C'mon in!"

One by one, the group stepped into the large motor home. Concord had never been inside one, so he was excited to see what it looked like. It was almost like stepping into a small apartment. Just inside the door was a kitchen along one side and a table along the other. Farther back, there were a couple of large comfortable chairs and a couch. Beyond the couch was a small hallway that led to a bathroom and a bedroom.

Two mechanics sat at the table. Both men wore dark blue mechanic uniforms. One man was tall and had a dark moustache. The other was short and wore an old blue bandana tied around his head. In front of each man was a cup of coffee.

"Hi folks," the tall mechanic said. "You caught us on our coffee break."

"Nice motor home," Uncle Joe said as he looked around.

"Yeah, it's a real humdinger," the tall mechanic replied. "We just started working on it today. We're supposed to fix some transmission problems, but we thought we'd start the job with an inspection of the coffee pot, if you know what I mean," he said with a laugh. The short mechanic laughed, too. "Coffee anyone?" the short mechanic asked with another laugh.

The Cunninghams shook their heads, and so did the truck drivers. The tall mechanic noticed that his customers weren't laughing, so he got serious. "So, what can we do for you folks?" he asked.

"We're having some engine trouble," Archie said. He described the truck and its problems. "The truck is parked out on the street. Would you be willing to take a look?" "Sure thing," the tall mechanic said with a smile. He took one last drink of coffee and set down his mug. Then he turned to the other mechanic. "Let's go see what we can do," he said. The short mechanic nodded and stood up.

Concord suddenly realized that he was standing in the motor home's main walkway and was blocking everyone from getting out. So, he quickly spun around to leave. As he did, the side of his coat hit a bunch of large yellow bananas on a nearby counter. The bananas fell onto the floor. "I'm sorry," Concord said. He quickly reached down, picked them up, and put them back on the counter.

"Don't worry about it, kid," said the short mechanic. "Those aren't ours. And I think the owners of this motor home could afford some new bananas if anything happens to these," he said with a chuckle.

"Yeah, and that's what we figured about the coffee supply, too," the tall mechanic said. The two mechanics laughed again.

Mr. Cunningham shook his head as he turned and walked out of the motor home. Concord followed. After a few steps, Mr. Cunningham turned to Concord. "Concord, I hope you're more respectful of other people's things than what you saw in there," he whispered.

"For sure, Dad," Concord whispered back with a nod. "Do you think it's a good idea to ask these guys to work on the tree truck?"

"Good question," Mr. Cunningham whispered. "From what I've seen so far, I'm not sure they can be trusted. Unfortunately, Max and Archie may not have much of a choice. This truck needs to get back on the road if we're going to make it to Washington, D.C. on schedule. These mechanics might be the only ones in town, and I don't know if the truck could make it to the next town."

The group followed Concord and Mr. Cunningham through the open shop door and out to the street. When they got to the truck, Max climbed into the cab of the truck and pulled a lever, which released the hood. The short mechanic lifted the hood, and he and his partner began their evaluation. A few minutes later, they slammed the hood shut.

"Well, it looks like you've blown a gasket," the short mechanic said.

"How long would it take you to fix it?" Archie asked.

"We could probably get it done in about six hours," the tall mechanic said.

Mr. Cunningham began scribbling notes. Meanwhile, Uncle Joe took out his camera and took a picture of the repair shop.

"What's going on here?" the tall mechanic asked.

"We thought some folks might want to learn a little bit about the repair shop that helped keep the Capitol Christmas Tree on its way to Washington, D.C.," Mr. Cunningham said.

The short mechanic stepped back and looked at the tree on the trailer. "Do you mean that this tree is going to the United States Capitol building?" he asked.

"It sure is," Archie said. "And we don't have much spare time on our schedule. So, should we unhitch the trailer and bring the truck into the garage?" he asked.

The short mechanic nodded. He began to answer, "Sounds goo-" when the other mechanic slapped him on the shoulder.

"I think my partner has forgotten something," the tall mechanic said. He leaned over and whispered into the other mechanic's ear. Then he turned back to the group. "We promised the owner of the motor home that we would have his vehicle repaired within two weeks or we would do the repair for free. He brought the motor home to us two weeks ago tomorrow. So, we need to finish it by the end of the day tomorrow or we won't get paid for the job."

Mr. Cunningham looked up from his notepad. "But didn't you say earlier that you just started working on the motor home today?"

The tall mechanic nervously shifted his eyes to the left and then to the right. "That's right," he finally said. "We've been waiting for a part to be delivered. It's a good thing that the part came today. If we work real hard, we'll have just enough time to get the job done by the end of the day tomorrow. But, that means we won't have time to work on your truck for a couple of days." Then he shrugged and a small smile crept across his face. "Of course, if you're willing to pay enough money to cover both your repair and the motor home repair, we wouldn't need to worry about missing our deadline. Then we could fix your truck today."

Uncle Joe leaned over to Mr. Cunningham, "This sounds like a scam," he whispered. "Do you think he's just trying to get extra money?"

As Mr. Cunningham and Uncle Joe whispered back and forth, Archie and Max discussed the situation. And Concord dashed over to the van, opened his backpack, and grabbed his Bible.

After a minute of discussion, Archie decided that they didn't have much of a choice. He finally turned back to the mechanics. "Why don't you tell me what it will cost to cover both repairs," he said with disgust.

The tall mechanic smiled. He was just about to answer when Concord stepped forward with his Bible. Mr. Cunningham grinned, put his hand on Concord's shoulder, and nodded at his son.

"I don't think paying for both repairs will be necessary," Concord announced. His Bible was open and his finger was on a verse. "The motor home hasn't been here for two weeks. There should be enough time to repair the truck first and still finish the motor home before the two weeks are up."

"What are you talking about?" asked the tall mechanic. "Just ask my partner. That motor home has been locked up on our lot for one week and six days." He slapped his partner on the shoulder.

"Uh, that's right," the other mechanic said nervously.

"I think you'd both better read Revelation 14:15," the Scripture Sleuth replied. "I'm sure you'll agree that you're a little mixed up on your dates."

How does Concord know that the mechanics are lying?

Read Revelation 14:15 for the clue Concord gave the mechanics.

The solution to Breakdown Blues is on page 106.

10
THE JUMBO JUGGLERS

"Did I hear you say that the Jumbo Jugglers are in this morning's Thanksgiving Holiday Parade?" Mr. Cunningham asked the hotel clerk.

"That's right," the clerk said with a smile. The young clerk was tall and wore braces on her teeth. She handed Mr. Cunningham his receipt.

"I can't believe the Jumbo Jugglers are actually in town," he said. He smiled and shook his head with surprise. "I usually see them on TV, and they're always performing in parades in huge cities."

The Cunninghams were in a small town just off of Interstate 68 in Maryland.

"One of the jugglers grew up here, and he convinced the rest of the group to come perform in this year's parade," the clerk said.

Mr. Cunningham turned toward Concord and Faith. "Can you kids believe that?" he asked excitedly. "You get to see the Jumbo Jugglers in person today!"

"Uh, Dad," Concord said quietly. He looked over at Faith. She nodded. Then Concord looked back at his dad. "We've never heard of the Jumbo Jugglers."

"What?" Mr. Cunningham exclaimed. He turned back to the clerk. "Can you believe that?"

The clerk opened her mouth to answer, but Mr. Cunningham was so excited that he had already turned back to Concord. "Concord, the Jumbo Jugglers are these amazing jugglers who have been performing in parades for years."

"Why are they called the Jumbo Jugglers?" Faith asked.

"It's because of what they juggle," Mr. Cunningham answered. "Everything they use is bigger or heavier than what regular jugglers use. The last time I saw them, they were juggling folding lawn chairs."

"And the last time I saw them, they were juggling guitars," Uncle Joe added.

The more Concord and Faith heard about the Jumbo Jugglers, the more excited they were to see them.

Mr. Cunningham turned back to the clerk. "So where's the best place along the parade route to see the Jumbo Jugglers?" he asked.

"You'll want to be half way up the hill on Burnout Road," the clerk said. "That's where the parade judges are going to be."

"Won't that be a crowded place?" Faith asked.

"Oh yeah," the clerk agreed. "But if the judges are there, then all the performers will do their best shows right there." She pulled out a town map and circled the spot. Then she handed the map to Mr. Cunningham. "Even though we're a small town, this year's parade is sure going to be fantastic. You probably won't believe this, either, but the Capitol Christmas Tree is going to be in the parade, too!" she said with a proud smile.

The Cunninghams chuckled. "Now that we can believe," Mr. Cunningham said with a grin.

Mr. Cunningham thanked the clerk, and the group headed for the van. As they studied the town map, they realized that they were only a few blocks from the judges' booth. So, they decided to walk. They locked all their bags in the van, except for Concord's backpack, and they were off.

A couple of minutes later, they were turning a corner toward Burnout Road. Faith suddenly stopped and pointed at a parking lot down the street. "Hey everybody, look!" she cried out. The Cunningham Family stopped and looked down the street.

"That's a nice parking lot," Uncle Joe said with a confused tone.

"Keep watching, Dad, and you'll see something else," Faith said. About five seconds later, Uncle Joe saw what she was talking about. So did Concord and Mr. Cunningham. There were snow shovels flying into the air behind the cars!

"That must be the Jumbo Jugglers," Mr. Cunningham said with a smile. "I'll bet they're warming up for the parade."

"Should we go take a sneak peek?" Uncle Joe asked.

"You bet!" Mr. Cunningham said excitedly.

A minute later, the Cunninghams joined about fifty other people who had discovered the practice spot of the Jumbo Jugglers. The jugglers were scattered around the parking lot, practicing with their snow shovels.

A whistle blew, and the jugglers went to their positions. There were twenty-one of them, and they all wore green sweatshirts and red hats. Twenty of the jugglers stood in rows to start the routine. The last juggler, who seemed to be the leader, stood in front of the group.

"Okay everyone," the leader said into a megaphone. "Now we're going to practice our competition routine. This is the one that we'll do in front of the judges. Everybody ready?"

All the jugglers nodded. Then some fast-paced music

started playing from two huge speakers in the back of a pickup truck. The pickup was parked a few feet beyond the leader, and it would also be driving in front of the group in the parade. The leader waited a few beats, and then he threw one of his snow shovels twenty feet into the air.

"Whoa!" Concord exclaimed, along with most of the crowd.

The moment the leader's shovel came back down into his hands, the other jugglers each threw one of their snow shovels into the air and started their routines. The Cunninghams watched in amazement as the jugglers did all sorts of unbelievable stunts with their snow shovels and other items that they would grab out of the back of the pickup.

"I can see why you're so excited about seeing these guys," Concord said to his dad. "They're fantastic!"

Mr. Cunningham nodded and smiled.

After about three minutes of excitement, the jugglers finished their routine. The small crowd clapped wildly.

"Thank you folks," the leader said through the megaphone. "We'll be doing this again in front of the judges on Burnout Road. See you there!"

The crowd quickly broke up and began walking toward the parade route. The Cunninghams followed the crowd, and a few minutes later they were standing about twenty feet to the left of the judges' booth on Burnout Road. It was half-way up the hill, just as the hotel clerk had said.

"Good thing it's not snowing," Uncle Joe said as he looked at the street. The smooth pavement was steep enough to make it difficult for cars to climb if it was icy.

"If it snows, I know a few people with snow shovels who might be able to help," Mr. Cunningham joked. Then he looked up at the clear blue sky. "I don't think we'll have to worry about snow today, though."

Concord glanced toward the bottom of the hill and saw a marching band. The parade was starting, and he could sense the excitement in the crowd. People seemed to be pressing forward to the curb so they could see better.

As the marching band's music grew louder and the excitement built, a worried look came to Concord's face. He rubbed his chin as he thought. Then he tapped Faith on the shoulder. "Do you remember the jugglers' routine?" Concord asked.

"I think so," Faith said. "Do you mean the whole thing?"

Concord shook his head. "Just when they spun things on their elbows," he said.

"Oh yeah, I loved those tricks!" Faith said with a laugh. She closed her eyes and concentrated. "Okay, let me think. They started by spinning a shovel on one elbow. Then they stopped, and each juggler grabbed a bowling ball out of the back of the pickup. Then they spun a shovel on one elbow and a bowling ball on the other elbow."

"I still can't believe they were able to do that," Concord said.

Faith continued. "After that, they all set down their bowling balls on the parking lot and sat on them. They were sitting in a tight circle. They were facing outward so they could see the audience. Then they started balancing their shovels on their noses. They carefully stood up and slowly took eight or nine steps toward the audience. They kept the shovels balanced on their noses the whole time! Finally, they walked back to the circle of balls, picked them up, and they spun their balls on their elbows again. And they were still balancing the shovels on their noses!"

Concord nodded. "Thanks, Faith," he said. Then he sighed.

"Is something wrong?" Faith asked.

"There will be," Concord said. "Something is going to go wrong with the Jumbo Jugglers' routine," Concord said.

"How do you know?" Faith asked. She looked at Concord's backpack. He hadn't unzipped it.

Concord tapped the side of his head. "I've been working on memorizing Bible passages during the trip," he said. He dropped his backpack to the ground and pulled out his Bible. He opened it to chapter sixteen of the book of Mark and handed the Bible to Faith. "Here, read Mark 16:4," The Concordance said. "I've got to ask my dad if there's a way to warn the Jumbo Jugglers!"

What will go wrong with the Jumbo Jugglers' routine?

Read Mark 16:4 to read the clue Concord gave Faith.

The solution to Jumbo Jugglers is on page 107.

11
WELCOME TO
WASHINGTON D.C.

"I can't believe we're finally here!" Concord said excitedly. The semi with the tree was about to enter Washington, D.C., and the Cunninghams' van was right behind it. "Do you think anyone is expecting the tree's arrival today?" Concord asked.

"I think you could say that," Mr. Cunningham said. He was leaning his head against the van window and looking past the tree truck. Then he smiled and said, "You're not going to believe this!"

Just as they reached the official city limits of Washington, D.C., four police cars quickly surrounded the semi and turned on their flashing lights. Another four motorcycle policemen drove in from a side street and joined the group. All the officers gave a nod and a smile to the truck drivers, and they motioned for the semi to follow them.

"The tree truck is getting a police escort!" Concord cried out. "Cool!"

With lights flashing and sirens sometimes blaring, the police guided the Capitol Christmas Tree through the busy streets of Washington, D.C. Though the Cunninghams weren't officially part of the police escort, Mr. Cunningham did a nice job of keeping up. A short time later, the short parade arrived at the grounds of the U.S. Capitol building.

The police told Max and Archie to park the semi right along the curb in front of the Capitol grounds. Mr. Cunningham knew that he had to find an actual parking spot, so he began nervously scanning the street.

Faith was already on the job. "There's going to be a parking spot right over there," she said, pointing toward a large delivery van. Mr. Cunningham didn't see anything at first. But a few seconds later, the driver of the delivery van hopped into his seat and pulled into traffic. There was a perfect spot suddenly available.

"Great job, Faith!" Mr. Cunningham said with relief.

As soon as the Cunningham van was in the parking spot, Uncle Joe jumped out his door and began snapping pictures. The view of the tree on the semi with the U.S. Capitol in the background was fantastic.

Mr. Cunningham quickly grabbed his notepad off the dashboard and turned to Concord and Faith. "Let's go join the fun," he said with a smile. They all put on their coats, Concord grabbed his backpack, and they jumped out of the van. By the time they made it to the tree truck, Max and Archie had already climbed down from their seats. They were being greeted with smiles and handshakes by the policemen.

"Congratulations, gentlemen, for safely bringing the tree all the way across the country," a police officer said to Max and Archie, "and thanks for your radio call to our dispatcher." He was tall and muscular, and he wore a dark blue police uniform. "I'm Captain Adams. On behalf of the entire police force, I want to let you know that it was our pleasure to escort you and the nation's Christmas tree on the last few miles of your journey."

"Thank you," said Max, who had been driving. "I didn't realize we were going to get a police escort until all of you joined us and started flashing your lights." Then he smiled at all the officers. "I was just glad I wasn't being pulled over."

The police officers all laughed. Captain Adams gave Max a slap on the back. "Would you like to see where they're going to put the tree?" he asked Max and Archie.

Both drivers nodded, and the group began walking across the Capitol grounds. Mr. Cunningham, Concord, and Faith followed. Uncle Joe told them he would join them later; he was going to try to get to the top of a nearby office building and take more pictures.

After walking for a couple of minutes, the three Cunninghams and the rest of the group stood around a hole in the middle of the Capitol lawn. The hole was about six feet deep, and it was just wide enough to hold the enormous tree trunk.

Concord and Faith had worked their way to the front of the group so they could see the hole. While the drivers and the police were talking, Faith knelt to the ground and looked into the hole.

"Did anyone see that envelope down there?" she asked. Concord was the only one who was paying attention to her.

"An envelope?" he asked.

"Take a look," Faith said as she pointed down the hole.

Concord knelt beside her and looked into the hole. "You're right," he said with interest. Then he lowered his head a little further. "And it says something about the Capitol Christmas Tree." Concord looked up at the drivers and the police. They were still talking. So, he decided to tap his dad on the arm.

"Hey, Dad," Concord whispered. "There's an envelope in the hole."

"It's probably just some garbage that blew in there," Mr.

Cunningham answered.

"It doesn't look like garbage," Concord replied. "Will you take a look?"

Mr. Cunningham decided that he could spare a moment, so he took three steps over to the edge of the hole. He bent down and looked in. He saw the envelope, and he saw the words "Capitol Christmas Tree." But he couldn't read the other words. So, he pulled out his key ring, which had a small flashlight attached to it. He shined the light down the hole, took a look, and then he froze.

"What is it?" Concord asked.

"Hang on," he replied.

Mr. Cunningham quickly stood up and turned toward the policemen. "Excuse me, officers," he said rather loudly. Most of them stopped talking and turned toward him. "Would you be willing to take a question from the press?"

Captain Adams smiled. "Sure thing," he said.

"Has anyone been threatening to damage the tree?" Mr. Cunningham asked.

Captain Adams chuckled. "Of course not," he said with a smile. "They know we'd track them down and arrest them if they tried to pull off something like that." Then the smile dropped from his face. "Why do you ask?"

"I think you'd better look down the hole," Mr. Cunningham answered.

Captain Adams stepped over to the edge of the hole. Then he pulled a flashlight from a pouch attached to his belt. He turned on the flashlight and looked down the hole. He stood there for a moment. Then he turned toward one of his officers. "Officer Smith, grab my feet!" he shouted. Officer Smith hurried over to Captain Adams and grabbed his feet. "Don't let go!" Captain Adams ordered. A second later, Captain Adams dove into the hole! It was just wide enough for his body. Officer Smith gave Captain Adams a few seconds to grab the envelope, and then he pulled him up and out of the hole. Captain Adams had the envelope in his hand.

Concord and Faith looked at the envelope and then looked at each other. They finally saw the rest of the words on the front of the envelope. The words said, "Capitol Christmas Tree will be destroyed. Open for details."

Concord was glad he had grabbed his backpack when they left the van. His Bible was in the pack, and he knew it might come in handy.

Captain Adams opened the envelope and read the letter aloud. He read, "Hello. My name is Dr. Toxic. I poisoned the Capitol Christmas Tree four months ago while it was still growing near Pine Tops. The poison will make the tree turn black ten days from now unless the tree receives the medicine it needs. I created the poison, and I am the only one who knows what medicine will save the tree. If the Capital Christmas Tree doesn't receive the medicine, it will become uglier than you could ever imagine."

Max and Archie gasped. Mr. Cunningham stood there, stunned.

"Wasn't the location of the tree a secret until about a week ago?" asked Uncle Joe.

Mr. Cunningham nodded. "It was a secret to the general public," he said. "But there were quite a few people in the forest service who knew its location."

Captain Adams continued. He read, "I will give you the medicine to save the tree if you pay me $50,000. At the bottom of this note is the number of a bank account in Switzerland. Deposit the money there."

"This has got to be a joke, right?" Max asked with a worried look on his face.

"There's more," Captain Adams said. He read, "Do you need proof? Find a tree expert. Then go look under the bench that is fifty yards west of this hole."

Every head in the group looked up and to the west. There, across the grounds, was a bench. And there was indeed something under it. One of the officers ran to the bench to get the item.

Meanwhile, Captain Adams finished the note. He read, "In the box under the bench is a tree branch that I clipped from the tree when I poisoned it. I clipped this sample of the tree to prove to you that I really was with the tree. Your tree expert will be able to tell you that the branch in the box is an exact match with the Capitol Christmas Tree. Have the expert use a microscope. You'll see that the cells and even the DNA are identical. Don't expect your tree expert to find the poison, though. I made sure the poison will stay invisible until it's too late. Don't ruin Christmas for America. Pay the money. Signed, Dr. Toxic."

The officer who had run to the bench was back, and he handed the box to Captain Adams. Captain Adams ripped it open and pulled out the branch. Then he yelled, "C'mon!" He ran toward the tree truck, and everyone followed.

After a quick sprint across the grounds, the group was standing next to the tree truck. Captain Adams held up the branch next to the tree. The needles on the branch were the same length, width, shape, and color as the branches on the tree. It looked like an exact match. Captain Adams shook his head with frustration. And Concord pulled his Bible out of his backpack.

"Sir," one of the officers said. "Should I go find a tree expert?"

"Yes," Captain Adams said. "On the double. We need

to confirm this is a match."

The officer hurried off to his patrol car and began making calls.

"Sir," another officer said. "What if this Dr. Toxic guy just clipped a branch from the tree and stuck it in the box. Maybe he never poisoned the tree, and this is all just a trick to get $50,000."

"You could be right," Captain Adams replied. "But what if you aren't? What if Dr. Toxic is telling the truth and this tree is going to turn black right in the middle of the Christmas season. Can we risk it?"

Concord stepped forward. "I think you can," he said.

"Not now, kid," Captain Adams said. "We might have a disaster on our hands."

Concord looked down at the Bible in his hands. "I think I can prove that you don't," he said.

"What?" Captain Adams replied.

"If you'll allow me to read John 15:6," The Concordance said, "I think you'll see that Dr. Toxic's note is a lie."

How can Concord be certain that Dr. Toxic's note isn't true?

Read John 15:6 for the clue that Concord gave Captain Adams.

The solution to Welcome to Washington, D.C. is on page 108.

12
BIG BOUNCE SHOES

"There it is!" Concord announced. He was pressing his nose against the airplane window. The Cunninghams had just taken off from Washington, D.C., and Concord was enjoying a perfect view of the Capitol Christmas Tree below.

"I guess that's one good thing about taking such an early morning flight," Mr. Cunningham said as he leaned over to take a look. "It's still so dark outside that we can see all the beautiful lights on the tree. What a great way to start the morning."

"Are you sure that it's actually morning?" Concord joked as he yawned. "It feels like the middle of the night." As the plane rose above the clouds, Concord leaned back against his seat and slowly closed his eyes.

The Cunninghams had been up very late last night. There had been a big ceremony for the lighting of the tree. After that, there was a party for everyone who had been a part of the tree project. The Cunninghams finally returned to their hotel at about midnight, and they had to wake up to go to the airport just four hours later.

Though they were all tired, they were happy to be on their way home. Their journey from Pine Tops to Washington, D.C. had been a great success. Mr. Cunningham had sent back many interesting stories to the *Ponderosa Press*. Uncle Joe had sent back just as many fantastic pictures. Concord and Faith had enjoyed seeing many parts of the country for the first time, and Concord's Scripture sleuthing had solved many mysteries along the way.

Concord slept so well on the airplane that his eyes didn't open until they were almost to Denver. As the plane slowed down to land, Concord lifted his head off the back of his seat and looked around. "How long have I been sleeping?" he asked as he rubbed his eyes.

"You just slept halfway across the country," Mr. Cunningham answered.

"I guess that's one half down, and one half to go," Concord joked as he stretched his arms.

They landed a few minutes later. The Cunninghams exited the plane and walked up the enclosed ramp to the airport. After waiting in the airport for an hour, they boarded their next flight. This one would take them from Denver to Seattle. After arriving in Seattle, they switched planes once more.

For their final flight they were on a smaller airplane with propellers. The flight was smooth, and after about an hour they landed on the airstrip at the tiny Pine Tops Airport. The airplane door opened, and everyone stood up to get off.

The Cunninghams had been sitting at the front of the airplane, so they were the first people out the door. This time there was no enclosed ramp; they had to climb down metal stairs and then walk across part of the runway to get to the airport.

Concord took a deep breath as he went down the stairs. "Yep," he said with a grin. "Smells like home!"

The Cunninghams all chuckled. After all four of them were off the stairs, they began walking toward the airport together. They were about half way to the building when Chief Riggins and two of his deputies came bursting out the airport door.

"Hi Chief!" Mr. Cunningham shouted with a big wave.

"Cunninghams?" the chief said with surprise. He paused for a brief moment, and then he rushed over to meet them. The deputies followed. "Welcome home!" he said. "Were you on this flight?" he asked.

"Sure thing, Chief," Mr. Cunningham said. "This one, and two others before it."

"This is the only one that I'm interested in," the chief said. "It's the reason my deputies and I are here. I hope we're not too late. Were you folks the first people off the plane?" the chief asked.

They all nodded. The chief motioned to his two deputies, who then walked over to the bottom of the stairs and waited for the other passengers to come down. For some reason, no one else had come off the airplane yet.

"What's going on, Chief?" Mr. Cunningham asked.

The chief leaned in toward the Cunninghams. "There may have been a robber on that flight," he said quietly.

"A what?" Faith said as her eyes bulged.

Mr. Cunningham and Uncle Joe quickly felt their back pockets to see if they still had their wallets. Concord dropped his backpack to the ground, opened it up, and checked to see if all of his things were still there. No one seemed to be missing anything.

The chief shook his head. "I'm not talking about a robbery on the plane," he said. "The Seattle police just called me. There was a robbery in Seattle a couple of hours ago. The robber stole some secret shoes from a Seattle company's research office, and then he managed to get away. But the police think he was on this flight."

Mr. Cunningham reached into his coat pocket and whipped out his reporter's notepad. He had been home less than a minute and he was already back to work. "Excuse me, Chief. Did you say secret shoes?" Mr. Cunningham asked.

The chief nodded. "A company over there invented a new shoe with a special design," the chief quickly explained. "They claim it can help people jump twice as high as they can with regular shoes. They call the shoe the Big Bounce."

"I suppose the shoes are worth lots of money," Uncle Joe said.

"About two thousand dollars per pair," the chief replied. "And the robber stole ten pairs of them!"

"How do they know he was on this flight?" Mr. Cunningham asked.

Before Chief Riggins answered, he lifted his chin and looked over Mr. Cunningham's shoulder. The next two people coming out of the airplane were older ladies, and one of them had a walking cane. The ladies were slowly making their way down the steps, and they were holding up the line. The chief turned back to the group.

"Well," the chief said, "after the robber got away, the Seattle police were looking everywhere for him. There was a problem, though. The robber was never seen, so the police had no idea what he looked like. But they caught a break. They sent a bulletin with the details of the robbery to all the places they thought the robber might go. They received a phone call from a security officer at the airport. She told the police that she had seen a suitcase full of strange looking shoes."

"She saw them?" Mr. Cunningham repeated as he wrote in his notepad.

"Well, sort of," the chief replied. "She was working at the spot where you put your carry on bags through the X-ray machine. She remembered seeing the strange shoes in an X-ray picture of one of the bags she had scanned."

"Why didn't she tell the police right when she saw the shoes?" Faith asked.

The chief looked over Mr. Cunningham's shoulder again. The elderly ladies were still trying to get down the stairs from the airplane. And they were still holding up the line. The chief turned back to the Cunninghams. "She didn't report it right away because she was looking for dangerous things like guns and knives. There's nothing wrong with taking shoes on a plane."

"Unless they're stolen," Mr. Cunningham said.

"Right," the chief said with a nod.

"So how did the police figure out that the robber was on our plane?" Mr. Cunningham asked.

"They looked at the recordings from the airport security cameras," Chief Riggins said. "There are cameras recording everything that happens at the security spot as well as the rest of the airport. The police were able to figure out which suitcase the shoes were in by reviewing the security tapes. Then they checked tapes from another angle to see who the suitcase belonged to. After that, they looked through all the other security tapes in the airport to see which flight the robber took. They said he got onto this flight."

"Do you have a picture of the robber?" Mr. Cunningham asked.

"The Seattle police are sending it to our police station right now," the chief said. "I didn't have time to go there first to pick it up. But, the Seattle police told me that the robber should be easy to spot because of the suitcase with the shoes. It's a new red suitcase."

"So is that what you're watching for now?" Mr. Cunningham asked.

The chief nodded.

"Uh, Chief?" Uncle Joe said. "What if there are two people on the flight that carried on new red suitcases?"

The chief's eyebrows tightened for a moment. "Good question," he said. Then his face brightened. "I almost forgot. The police said that the robber was also carrying a second suitcase. We're guessing that it's loaded with stolen stuff, too. They didn't say what color it was, but I guess it's pretty beat up and slightly bigger than the red suitcase."

"So we're looking for a man with a new red suitcase and an older second suitcase," Mr. Cunningham said as he scribbled in his notepad.

The group turned and looked at the stairs. The two elderly ladies had finally reached the bottom, and the line of people behind them began to move. One by one, the other passengers stepped off the airplane. The Cunninghams, the chief, and the two deputies studied the suitcases that each person carried off the plane.

After a couple of minutes there was a pause, and then the flight attendants and pilots came down the stairs.

The chief rushed over to the flight attendants. "Is that everyone?" he asked nervously.

"That's it," the flight attendant answered.

Not one person who came off the plane had been carrying a new red suitcase, or a red suitcase of any kind. The chief rubbed his chin. "Is it possible that the Seattle police made a mistake?" he asked his deputies. "Maybe the robber wasn't on this flight."

The chief gasped as a thought came to him. "The robber must have seen us out here," he mumbled to himself.

"He probably left the red suitcase on the plane." Chief Riggins pointed at his deputies and then pointed at the airplane. "Quick, search the plane!" he exclaimed. "The suitcase must still be inside!"

The deputies ran up the stairs and began searching the plane. Meanwhile, Concord dropped his backpack to the ground and began a search of his own in his Bible.

While the deputies were searching the airplane, the chief asked the flight attendants if the robber could drop anything out of the airplane while it was in the air. They said that was impossible. There would have been all sorts of alarms if any doors or hatches had been opened.

A couple of minutes later, the deputies still hadn't come out of the airplane.

"I expected them to find the suitcase by now," the chief said. "I'd better go give them some help."

A few minutes later, the chief and his deputies came back out of the airplane. The chief sighed. "I don't understand," he said. "We searched every inch of that plane. There's no red suitcase in there."

"If the suitcase isn't on the airplane, and it didn't come off the airplane, where could it be?" Uncle Joe asked.

Concord looked up from his Bible. "I think I know," he said. "I think the robber got away with the suitcase."

Chief Riggins shook his head. "How is that possible?" he asked. "Did he paint the suitcase a different color?"

"He didn't need to," Concord said. Then he held out his Bible to the group. "Try reading Matthew 9:17. Maybe you'll see what I mean."

How did the robber get away with the suitcase?

Read Matthew 9:17 for the clue that Concord gave the group.

The solution to Big Bounce Shoes is on page 109.

Solutions

Solution to Chapter One: The Painted Pine

In John 4:11, a woman wonders how Jesus will get water out of a deep well because he has nothing to lift the water. Concord realized that Mr. Dudley also had nothing to carry water from the stream. The only things he had with him that could possibly carry water were his tennis shoes, but Faith confirmed that they weren't wet.

Concord also knew that there was nothing else around for Mr. Dudley to use. There were no buildings to look through. At the time the supposed tree rescue took place, there would have been no cars there. Also, Mr. Dudley had said that the man with the paint had taken his paint can with him when he fled, so that wasn't a possibility either.

After Concord told his dad the flaw in Mr. Dudley's story, Mr. Cunningham asked Mr. Dudley how he managed to carry the water. Without answering, Mr. Dudley ran away as fast as he could. But he couldn't get away before Uncle Joe took a close-up picture of his face. The *Ponderosa Press* gave copies to all the other reporters and told them the man in the picture could never be trusted.

Solution to Chapter Two: The City Sign Bandit

In Acts 22:11, Paul explains how he was not able to see because a great light had blinded him. In a similar way, when it's dark and a bright light is shining in a person's face, it's hard for that person to see anything else. Concord remembered that Mr. Cain had claimed to see the hood ornament of the City Sign Bandit when the bandit's truck passed him on the highway.

However, in Mr. Cain's story, the trucks passed each other while going down a dark forest highway at night. So their headlights would have been on. Mr. Cain would not have been able to see the hood ornament of the bandit's truck because of the brightness of the bandit's headlights. Therefore, Mr. Cain's story could not be true.

When the chief realized that Mr. Cain was lying, he immediately arrested him. The next day, police searched Mr. Cain's garage and found eighteen other signs, as well as a different truck with a stop sign hood ornament.

Solution to Chapter Three: The Disappearing Dog Walker

Jeremiah 7:24 talks about people going backward. Concord realized that the person who left the footprints in the cement must have walked backward when he left the restroom. By stepping in his original footprints, he would have avoided making a second set of footprints. Also, he must have carried his dog when he did it. It would then look like he and the dog went into the restroom but never came back out.

After trudging through the wet cement and opening the door, the construction worker was disappointed to discover that the man had indeed gotten away. However, he was thankful that Concord figured out what happened. Concord was very thankful when Faith walked around the corner and told him there was a women's restroom on the other side of the building. The cashier waited for the women's restroom to be empty, and then he stood guard while all the men in the group walked in to use it. Except for Concord. He ran in.

Solution to Chapter Four: The Ice Fish Shack

Job 41:1 refers to pulling a leviathan out of the water with a fishhook (or hook). Concord knew that if the fish had been caught in the mountain lakes, they would have been caught with fishhooks. However, the fish stolen from the hatchery were scooped out of the water with a net.

Therefore, Concord realized that one way to tell if the fish were caught at the lakes would be to look closely at their mouths. If their mouths had holes or cuts from fishhooks, the fish were caught at the lakes. If there were no holes, the fish would have been caught with a net.

After carefully inspecting the fish delivered to the restaurant, the biologist discovered that the fish had no fishhook holes, cuts, or marks in their mouths. When shown the evidence, the Ice Fish Shack fishermen confessed to their crime.

The Ice Fish Shack immediately hired new fishermen who actually caught their fish in the mountain lakes. The fish tasted twice as good, and business at the Ice Fish Shack suddenly exploded.

Solution to Chapter Five: The Super Spill

In Luke 22:31, Jesus refers to wheat being sifted. Concord realized that a creating a giant sift could quickly separate the golf ball-sized balls from the baseball-sized balls.

When Concord remarked that he was glad the drainage pit project was behind schedule, it was because the chain link fence hadn't yet been installed. He realized that the bundles of chain link fencing could be unrolled and stretched over the top of one of the trailers. The backhoe could then scoop up balls and dump them on top of the fencing. The small balls would fall through and into the trailer. The large balls would remain on top of the fencing and could be quickly scooped into the other trailer.

After the truck was on its wheels and the group did some "sifting," the driver made it to the factory two minutes before his deadline.

Solution to Chapter Six: Taste Test Troubles

Job 37:10 refers to ice, or frost, depending on your translation. Concord realized that Mr. Carson had left the Fresh Zap bottle out in the cold on the roof of his car. It was there from evening until the middle of the night. As Faith had remembered from the weather report, the temperature had been well below freezing all week. So, the water would have frozen in the bottle.

When water freezes, it expands. Because each water bottle had been filled up to the bottom of its cork, the expanding ice would have pushed the Fresh Zap cork right out of the bottle.

Sure enough, Concord and the group went out to Mr. Carson's car and found the cork on the ground beside the driver side door.

Mr. Carson was so grateful that he wrote down the Cunninghams' address and promised to send them a case of the new bottled water as soon as his company began selling it. The water arrived six months later, just in time for the hot summer days.

Solution to Chapter Seven: Lamp Love

2 Kings 6:4 refers to cutting down trees (or wood). Concord realized that Mr. Clark was planning to block Wildwood Lane by cutting down one or more of the trees alongside it. The tree or trees would fall across the road, and cars would not be able to get through.

Aunt Nancy would be forced to turn around and take the long way to the church. Or she could wait for the tree to be removed. Either way, she would miss her chance to bid on the lamp since Mr. Clark arranged for it to be the first item sold.

The next morning, Aunt Nancy left two hours early and took the long way to the church. Mr. Clark was shocked to see Aunt Nancy at the auction. After an intense bidding war, Mr. Clark won the lamp.

However, Mr. Clark called Aunt Nancy the day after the auction and asked her if she was interested in buying the lamp from him. He needed money. An eye witness to the tree chopping had reported his license plate to the police. The police then made Mr. Clark pay a road crew to remove the tree.

To make up for his misdeeds, Mr. Clark offered Aunt Nancy a great price on the lamp. She accepted the offer and his apology.

Solution to Chapter Eight: The Great Turtle Race

Mark 13:16 speaks of no one going back for a cloak or coat. In this case, if Mr. Kelly's story was true, he would not have had the chance to go back to the turtle pen to get his vest before bringing Turbo to the racetrack.

Mr. Kelly said that when he left to get a drink of water, Turbo was resting on his vest. According to his story, Mr. Kelly never went back to the turtle pen. However, when Mr. Kelly brought Turbo to the racetrack for his introduction, Mr. Kelly was wearing the vest. He even pulled a turtle treat out of his vest pocket when he handed Turbo to Mrs. Parker.

Mr. Kelly was forced to admit that he was lying. He then confessed that he was the one who had switched Turbo with a lookalike. Turbo was found in Mr. Kelly's car near the backdoor a few minutes later.

Mrs. Parker decided that Turbo was too upset about the turtlenapping to run in another race. Dudley was disqualified because Mr. Kelly was his owner. So, Max Jr. was declared the winner of the Great Turtle Race!

Solution to Chapter Nine: Breakdown Blues

Revelation 14:15 speaks of the harvest of earth being ripe. Concord remembered that the bananas he knocked off the counter in the motor home were yellow. However, the mechanics claimed that the motor home had been sitting in their parking lot for two weeks, waiting to get repaired.

Concord realized that if that was true, the bananas would have been ripening during those two weeks. They would have been black by now.

Concord's detective work forced the mechanics to admit they had lied about the motor home. They offered to fix the tree truck right away, and for a fair price. When the work was completed, the truck seemed to be back to normal. However, Max and Archie decided to have the truck inspected by a mechanic in the next town. Fortunately, the repair had been done correctly.

Solution to Chapter Ten: The Jumbo Jugglers

Mark 16:4 refers to the stone in front of Jesus' tomb being rolled away. Concord realized that the Jumbo Jugglers' bowling balls were going to roll away from them during their performance.

Part of their routine included all of the jugglers sitting on their bowling balls and then standing up and walking away from them. Since the jugglers would be performing on a hill, the balls would start rolling downhill when left alone!

Concord told his dad, who was able to get word to the Jumbo Jugglers before they did their routine for the judges. The jugglers changed their routine and simply carried their balls with them after sitting on them.

The Cunninghams laughed with relief when they saw the group that was marching behind the Jumbo Jugglers in the parade. It was a group of clowns on stilts, who would have been knocked over like bowling pins when the bowling balls came rolling down the hill.

Solution to Chapter Eleven: Welcome to Washington, D.C.

John 15:6 refers to a branch withering or drying up. Dr. Toxic claimed that he poisoned the tree four months ago. For proof, he claimed that when he poisoned the tree he clipped the branch that was in the box. Concord realized that if the branch in the box had been removed from the Capitol Christmas Tree four months ago, it would have dried up. However, the group had observed that needles on the branch were a perfect match with the tree. Even the color was the same. That would not be the case if the branch was dried up.

The mysterious Dr. Toxic was never captured, but the Capitol Christmas Tree stayed a beautiful shade of green for the entire time it stood on the Capitol grounds.

To thank Concord, Captain Adams ordered two of his men to give the Cunninghams a police escort to their hotel later that day.

Solution to Chapter 12: Big Bounce Shoes

Matthew 9:17 describes putting something new into something old (wine into wineskins or containers). The verse helped Concord realize that the robber placed the new red suitcase into the older, slightly bigger second suitcase.

Usually suitcases are full. However, the robber's second suitcase was empty, so he was able to put the red suitcase inside of it after he boarded the airplane. When the robber got off the airplane, the police and the Cunninghams were looking for the red suitcase. So, the robber was able to walk right by them without being noticed.

Though the robber escaped that day, he was arrested two weeks later when he and his friends won a local basketball tournament. The robber's team had so many rebounds and slam dunks that the officials decided to inspect the team's shoes, which turned out to be the missing Big Bounce sneakers.

Concord's
Secret

If your Bible has a Concordance, it will usually be found at the back of the book. It is a collection of the most common words found in the Bible, with their most used examples in the text under the word. Sometimes there is a brief description of what the word means. Learning how to use a Concordance gives a Bible scholar a marvelous tool for finding God's Truth on any subject in His Holy Word.

Below are a few examples of words found in the Concordance. Read them for practice, look up the verses, and you will see how much fun it is to do your own Scripture Sleuthing. Then get your Bible and you will be able to solve your own mysteries in life.

Appearance - brightness, radiance, sight
I Samuel 16:7, man looks at the outward *appearance*
Matthew 6:16, for they neglect their *appearance*
Matthew 28:3, his *appearance* was like lightning

Friend -
Proverbs 17:17, a *friend* loves at all times
Proverbs 18:24, a *friend* who sticks closer than a brother
John 15:13, lay down his life for his *friend(s)*

Impossible -
Matthew 19:26, with men this is *impossible*
Luke 1:37, nothing will be *impossible* with God

Money - gain
Ecclesiastes 5:10, who loves *money* will not be satisfied
Mark 6:8, no *money* in their belt
I Timothy 3:3, free from the love of *money*
Luke 19:23, why ....not put the *money*.....bank

Parents -
Matthew 10:21, children will rise up against *parents*
Romans 1:30, disobedient to *parents*
Ephesians 6:1, children, obey your *parents*

Sword -
Genesis 3:24, flaming *sword* which turned
Psalm 57:4, their tongue, a sharp *sword*
Ephesians 6:17, the *sword* of the spirit
Proverbs 5:4, sharp as a two-edged *sword*

Glad -
Matthew 5:12, rejoice and be *glad*
Proverbs 10:1, wise son makes a father *glad*
2 Corinthians 11:19, bear with the foolish *gladly*

Serpent -
Genesis 3:1, Now the *serpent* was more crafty
Psalm 58:4, venom of a *serpent*
John 3:14, Moses lifted up the *serpent* in the wilderness.
Matthew 10:16, be shrewd as *serpents*

Trouble - distress, affliction
I Kings 20:7, see how this man is looking for *trouble*
Job 5:6, does *trouble* sprout from the ground?
Psalm 9:9, a stronghold in times of *trouble*
Proverbs 10:10, who winks the eye causes *trouble*